A BEGINNER'S GUIDE TO THE

Deep Culture
Experience

A BEGINNER'S GUIDE TO THE

Deep Culture
Experience

Beneath the Surface

JOSEPH SHAULES

INTERCULTURAL PRESS

an imprint of Nicholas Brealey Publishing

BOSTON • LONDON

First published by Intercultural Press, an imprint of Nicholas Brealey
Publishing, in 2010.

20 Park Plaza, Suite 1115A	3-5 Spafield Street, Clerkenwell
Boston, MA 02116, USA	London, EC1R 4QB, UK
Tel: + 617-523-3801	Tel: +44-(0)-207-239-0360
Fax: + 617-523-3708	Fax: +44-(0)-207-239-0370
www.interculturalpress.com	www.nicholasbrealey.com

Printed in the United States of America

14 13 12 11 10 1 2 3 4 5

ISBN: 978-0-9842471-0-3

Library of Congress Cataloging-in-Publication Data

Shaules, Joseph.
    A beginner's guide to the deep culture experience : beneath the
surface / Joseph shaules.
        p. cm.
    Includes bibliographical references and index.
    ISBN 978-0-9842471-0-3
    1. Intercultural communication.   2. Multicultural education.
3. Language and languages—Study and teaching.   I. Title.
    P94.6.S479 2010
    303.48'2 22
                                        2010007373

CONTENTS

Contents

Contents

ADAPTIVE DEMANDS

RESISTANCE

ACCEPTANCE

ADAPTATION

DEEP ADAPTATION AND IDENTITY

DEEP CULTURE LEARNING AND SELF-AWARENESS

Chapter Nine

Understanding Cultural Difference

SIMPLE UNIVERSALS

ASKING WHY

UNIVERSAL DILEMMAS

THE PITFALLS OF LABELING

Chapter Ten

Deep Culture, Clash, and Cash

CLASH

CULTURAL CONFLICT AND DIFFERENT REALITIES

DEEP CULTURE VERSUS CIVILIZATION

CASH

WHAT TO DO

Chapter Eleven

Personal Growth and Deep Culture Learning

ENGAGEMENT

RECONCILIATION

INNER AND OUTER

BREAKING ROUTINES

PLANNING THE JOURNEY

LANGUAGE LEARNING

ENTRY POINT

Contents

ACKNOWLEDGMENTS

A CONVERSATION WITH TORIKAI KUMIKO pushed me toward writing a book that makes a clear statement about what I believe rather than simply reporting on the thoughts of others. The format was inspired by Tom Verghese's wonderful book, *The Invisible Elephant: Exploring Cultural Awareness.* The first draft was born during a trip through Burgundy with Estelle Bisch, whose support and early feedback was critical. Many other people have provided detailed input and strong support, both by commenting on the manuscript and by supporting my work at the Japan Intercultural Institute and the Rikkyo Graduate School of Intercultural Communication. They include Daniela Arch, Janet Bennett, Florence Bourbon, Judy Carl, Alma Church, John Condon, Keiko Deshimaru, Joseph D'Souza, Cary Duval, Val Hansford, Ayako Hoshino, Travis Garcia, Ai Ichinomiya, Paul Jaffe, Gordon Jolley, Sumaiah El-Said, Masako Hiraga, Yukiko Ito, Cheryl Kirchhoff, Ellen Kawaguchi, Matthieu Kollig, Laurent Lepez, Adair Linn Nagata, Stefan Meister, Anne Niesen, Nobuo Nishikawa, Yoshimoto Oikawa, Mike Rost, Stephen Ryan, James Shaules, Pattie Shaules, Kumiko Torikai, Tom Verghese, Bob Whiting, Tomoko Yoshida, and (not least) Steve Ziolkowski. My largest debt goes to my son David, who, because of my peripatetic

lifestyle, has always had me around less than he should have.
I can only hope that what I have gained from my journeys
has enriched him in other ways. Thanks to all of you, and
to Antonio for getting me started.

CHAPTER ONE

Antonio
and the
Deep Culture
Journey

WHEN I WAS EIGHTEEN, I met a young man named Antonio on the main street of Ensenada, Mexico. He was only fifteen, but he was already helping to support his family by selling curios to American tourists. Hoping to practice my Spanish, I had crossed the border from San Diego and made my way south from Tijuana. On the street I struck up a conversation with Antonio. My Spanish was poor, and he was initially suspicious of my motives, but soon he opened up. This tiny success encouraged me, and I started heading to Ensenada whenever I had a chance. I saw Antonio again, and we became friends.

Though we were born only 100 kilometers (sixty-two miles) apart, Antonio and I lived in different worlds. I was American and he was Mexican. We spoke different languages and had radically different lives. And though our common interests were obvious enough—bicycles, sports, girls—getting to know Antonio made me feel that life as I experienced it was a geographical accident. Had I been born in his neighborhood in Mexico, I would have inhabited his reality instead of the one that I was familiar with. Seeing his life cast my life in a new light.

Taking a small step into Antonio's world had a subtle but profound impact on me. I decided to attend a three-month Spanish course in San Miguel de Allende, Guanajuato. There, I lived with a family and helped them run the family store. This experience opened my eyes to the difference between being a tourist and being a longer-term sojourner. Tourists are catered to by hotels, shuttle buses, and tour guides—an infrastructure that cushions them from the local community. As a resident, I had to adapt to my surroundings by getting to know the neighborhood, improving my Spanish, making new friends, and so on.

This was stressful but exciting. Learning Spanish changed me—I started to consider myself a Spanish speaker and felt connected to Mexico. I wanted to live there, not just visit. This led me to start a business and live for several years in the central Mexican city of Zacatecas. Eventually, I got itchy feet. I had the chance to move to Tokyo and took it. It was a big transition, but I became fascinated with my new home. I absorbed myself in the process of learning Japanese, working, and making a life for myself. Years later, I went to live in France and put myself through the adaptive process once again.

I owe Antonio a lot. His willingness to befriend me served as a catalyst for many later discoveries. I found that it's not easy to learn a foreign language or get used to life in a new country. Adapting to a new place involves learning the cultural outlook of your new home—how people think, what they value, what life means to them. And in the process of learning about other countries, I learned about myself. It is this process of self-discovery through cultural learning that this book focuses on.

THE CHALLENGE OF
CULTURAL LEARNING

This book is for sojourners—study-abroad students, expatriates, immigrants, or longer-term visitors—anyone who leaves home and spends a significant length of time in a new place. It's also for anyone who is interested in intercultural experiences. It focuses on the lessons we learn by exploring the cultural difference found in everyday life when living abroad. If we're honest with ourselves, we'll admit that despite modern conveniences, a stay in a foreign place is often no picnic. It can be stressful—even overwhelming. There's so much to learn and so many adaptations to make. It's easy to become irritable or frustrated as we get lost, struggle to communicate, and get unpleasant surprises. It's easy to lose perspective.

The most difficult challenges of this adaptive process—referred to in this book as *cultural learning*—are often the most hidden. We may expect trouble learning to eat strange food or dealing with noisy traffic in chaotic streets. But these relatively concrete things are often handled with surprisingly little difficulty. Frequently it's the more subtle things that are the bigger challenge—difficulties in communicating, trouble understanding what's expected of us, attitudes or behaviors that seem rude or inefficient. It's not a single incident or crisis that leads to this kind of stress—just an ongoing struggle to make sense of things and feel in control of our lives.

The psychological stresses of these adaptive challenges are sometimes referred to *culture shock*. This book attempts to see this stress in a new light. The difficulties that we face in a new environment can equally be seen as a precious learning opportunity. We are, first of all, learning about a new place—how to get along there. In addition to that, we have the chance to learn deeper lessons. A sojourn can bring to light hidden parts of one's cultural self and even provide insights into humans as cultural beings. A fundamental premise of this book is that a longer-term sojourn is the perfect opportunity for cultural and personal self-discovery.

Of course, we also learn cultural lessons without leaving home—we have books, information online and we're exposed to ethnic foods, music, and so on. We may have virtual connections to people who are far away—through social networks, for example. Our friends or colleagues may be from other countries. We may live in a border region or in a country with great cultural diversity. These things expand our view of the world. But when we are at home, we are less obliged to adapt—to change something about ourselves in order to get along. Abroad we face adaptive pressures—we're *obliged* to learn.

DEEP CULTURE

Spending even a day or a week in a new place can open our eyes to the world. But this book focuses on the cultural learning of longer sojourns because the concrete challenges of shorter stays (like unfamiliar streets or a bus station with signs we can't read) are more explicit and predictable. We deal with them consciously, and they can be planned for more easily. Longer stays involve more hidden challenges, such as learning new ways of communicating or thinking, and involve a deeper learning—one that touches upon the habits of our unconscious mind.

Cultural learning at this level revolves around the hidden programming of the mind called *deep culture*.[1] Deep culture influences our thinking and values in ways that we generally aren't aware of. We rely on it in everyday life to interact, communicate, and interpret others' actions. It is integrated into our thinking at such a basic level that we take it for granted. It is like water to a swimming fish and air to a flying bird. When we live abroad, we are like a fish pulled onto land—we are a bird that must swim. Patterns of thought and behavior that come naturally to us must be adjusted.

People who adapt deeply to life in a new country—especially if they must learn a foreign language to do so—often report transformational experiences like the one I had with Antonio. That's because longer sojourns bring us into contact with people who, despite our common humanity, have deep culture settings different from our own. Trying to make sense of these deep culture differences requires us to look beneath the surface and notice patterns of behavior and thought that are not obvious at first glance. And in the process of learning these deeper lessons about our cultural hosts, we bring to light previously hidden parts of ourselves.

I call this a *deep culture journey*. It involves a trial-and-error process of entering into another cultural reality—the world as seen from the point of view of our hosts. We gain a new perspective that can develop to the point that we feel that we have created a new self. We may even become bicultural. Some people experience this as a conscious shift between different selves and different social realities. They've created a new set of deep culture patterns in addition to the ones they grew up with.

ABOUT THIS BOOK

Many books about culture or life abroad make comparisons and generalizations about the people of particular places. In country X, do I shake hands, bow, or hug? This book, on the other hand, looks at deep culture and the experience of adapting to new cultural environments. It asks:

- What is the role of deep culture in everyday life?
- How can I gain a better understanding of deep culture?
- How can this understanding help me with the challenges of adapting while spending time abroad?
- How can I grow personally as a result of my journeys away from home?

The longer or more involved a sojourn, the more useful an awareness of deep culture is. Spending the day talking to Antonio taught me more than if I had simply wandered among the other American tourists. A summer studying Spanish in Mexico required adaptation, but learning to run a business there challenged me even more. But even when we aren't abroad or don't face these challenges, an awareness of deep culture is valuable in and of itself. When we do leave home, it can help us to get the most out of our sojourns—even when our away time is limited.

This book is called a "guide," but it doesn't give travel tips. Its goal is to give a tour of deep culture and cultural learning. We'll look at the idea of deep culture from different perspectives—intellectual, evolutionary, and historical. We'll start at home and see why we often don't notice deep culture in our everyday lives. We'll visit with the humans of prehistory to trace the evolutionary origins of deep culture. We'll look into cognition and the brain. We'll learn how thinking about culture has changed over time.

The latter part of the book focuses on the intercultural experiences we have during a sojourn. We will see how deep culture learning can be either *surface* or *deep*. And we will learn about *resistance*, *acceptance*, and *adaptation*—the three key elements to deep culture learning. We will also take a brief look at patterns of deep culture difference that we find around the world. And we will look at some ethical, social, and economic implications of our deep culture programming. Finally, we will look at the inner side of cultural learning, how we can grow personally from our sojourns.

Twenty-five years of living abroad and learning languages has utterly transformed my understanding of the human experience. What started as an interest in Spanish and life in Mexico has expanded to a curiosity about cultural diversity and the human mind. The journey of learning I began with Antonio is not over. I still struggle to understand cultural difference and the cultural programming of my own mind. But it's an exciting process. So why don't you join me as we explore the world of deep culture?

CHAPTER TWO

Deep Culture
in
Everyday Life

W HEN I FIRST TRAVELED TO MEXICO, I wasn't thinking about culture. I had trouble enough figuring out
which bus to board. If you had asked me to define culture,
I could only have produced vague images of the exotic
and ethnic: Balinese shadow puppets, the Taj Mahal, or a
stein of beer at Oktoberfest, perhaps. These were the kind
of images I found in the *National Geographic* magazines I
looked through as a child. I associated culture with civilization, ethnicity, and artistic creativity.

In my travels since then, I have seen many examples
of this kind of "exotic" culture. In Taipei, I saw a stun-
ning collection of the treasures of Chinese civilization. I've
climbed the Pyramid of the Sun in Teotihuacan, Mexico.
I've seen kimono-clad newlyweds sipping rice wine in a
Shinto wedding ceremony. I've seen Paris from the Eiffel
Tower, wandered through the Colosseum in Rome, and
bathed in a historic spa in Budapest. I've lost my way in
a maze-like souk in Marrakesh. On a beach in Thailand,
I watched as hundreds of paper box kites, with lit candles
inside, floated into the night sky to mark the New Year.

In spite of all this, these cultural experiences are not the ones that have left the greatest mark on me. Such experiences may be a reason to go abroad, but I don't think they are at the center of the intercultural experience. They seldom change us or affect our lives in important ways. Deeper cultural learning and transformation comes from an accumulation of reactions and adaptations—small things that we must deal with while attempting to get along in a new place. As we adapt to a new environment, our view of the world changes.

This book doesn't focus on the exotic, artistic, ceremonial, and visible parts of culture. We look at deep culture, or the cultural programming of the mind.[1] Deep culture has a profound impact on how we experience the world. "Deep" refers to the out-of-awareness nature of the patterns that have been socialized into us. These patterns give us a sense of what is normal—a sense that may not be shared by those living in other places.

I want to be careful about how I use the word culture because it can mean so many things. In its broadest sense, it refers to the learned things that groups of people share and pass on. In everyday language, we talk about someone being "cultured" to refer to his or her learning and refinement. Culture can also refer to a connection to a community—a way to describe one's heritage or ethnicity. When someone talks about being "proud of their culture," this is usually what they mean. I use the term deep culture in a more limited, specialized way. It refers to shared patterns of knowledge that our mind uses to create meaning and navigate our interaction with others.

This definition may sound a bit abstract. But you are, even at this moment, making use of unconscious patterns of knowledge as you read this. You need a vast network of linguistic and cultural knowledge to transform the marks on

FIGURE 2.1   What is culture?

this page into meaning. You may even hear these words in your head, as though I were speaking to you. You may read between the lines and gain a feeling for the type of person that I might be. You know whether this book is intended as fiction or nonfiction. You have a sense for the tone of my writing. All of these intuitions are built on patterns that have been internalized so efficiently that the magic of sharing a mental space with me seems commonplace.

Deep culture is like the operating system of the mind, and it usually goes unnoticed in our everyday lives. For example, if you are a U.S. American like me, when you go to a wedding and see a woman in a flowing white dress, you know that she is the bride. You know that white symbolizes purity. You understand that sex before marriage is traditionally considered impure in the traditional Christian view. You have an intuitive understanding of things like God, sin, and virtue. This knowledge is a natural part of automatically making sense of that white wedding dress.

In addition to—or because of—this shared background knowledge, you are able to make sense of what's happening at the wedding. You understand the vows being exchanged.

You can gauge who is dressed up and who isn't. You know the difference between formal interaction and more casual social exchanges. You make judgments based on this knowledge—that the decorations are extravagant, the musicians are playing badly, and that the family of the bride doesn't seem to like the family of the groom.

This knowledge is cultural because it is systematic and shared with others in the community. It is the ground against which we see objects and measure the meaning of things. It also guides your behavior. You know how far away to stand from someone when conversing at the reception. You greet your high school friend differently than you greet the bride's mother. You use *action chains*—sequences of behaviors you string together, such as shaking hands while you say, "How are you doing?" You engage in an ongoing dance of interaction and meaning making. All of this is made possible by deep culture programming that makes our day predictable and manageable—even boring. Its function is to provide an ongoing sense of what is normal.

At home, our sense of what's "normal" in everyday life is based on intuitions that we share with the people around us. You simply know whether a wedding, or someone's behavior, is typical, unusual, or weird. Have you ever felt uncomfortable around someone with a mental illness such as schizophrenia? This condition can give the impression to others that the sufferer is in a world of his or her own, or detached from reality. Yet the reality we are referring to is not physical reality, but the social reality of our community. The inability to participate in this shared reality is a crippling handicap.

The "normal" world that we share with others in our community is formed so automatically that it can be difficult to see how dependent we are on it. To understand it, we need to become aware of our own mental processes and unearth the hidden assumptions that already exist within us. Crossing borders and exploring the ways that others live and think can help us do this.

LAYERS OF DEEP CULTURE

Arriving in a new country, we often find that there are many things we already understand. The buildings, clothes, or shopping centers may seem much like they do back home. But if we stay a bit longer or look more closely, we begin to notice differences. People not only eat different foods and speak a different language—they think and act differently. The more interaction we have with this new place and its people, the more we realize that despite commonalities, things do not work in the new country the way they do back home. Because of this, it can be difficult to fully understand what things mean. To do so requires looking more deeply.

For example, visit Tokyo and you will see Japanese people bowing. Simple enough—you see that people seem to use it as a greeting. But there are deeper layers of meaning. Japanese bowing also reflects unconscious expectations and values. You may notice that some bows are deeper than others. People may even bow when talking on the phone. Certain expressions seem to go together with bowing. These subtleties hint at deeper layers of Japanese culture. There are, for example, hidden values related to using deference in order to create smooth human relations. These rest, in turn, on even more hidden cultural assumptions (for example, that hierarchy is a normal and potentially nurturing element of human interaction). What we see on the surface—the physical act of bending—in fact provides a window into many deeper layers of meaning.

A Japanese working with U.S. Americans, on the other hand, may find it striking that an American boss may permit employees to call her by her first name. Compared to the Japanese, Americans often speak casually to complete strangers. Again, there are layers of meaning beneath the surface behavior. The norms and values related to using first names rest on deep culture assumptions—for example, that informal behavior is friendlier than formal behavior, or that hierarchy in human relations is best avoided.

A French visitor to Japan told me that he had strong negative reactions to seeing Japanese bowing. It seemed to him unnaturally timid. He explained that in France bowing is associated with subservience in the face of royalty. These deep culture associations shaped his reaction to Japanese bowing. Similarly, a Japanese manager told me that U.S. American first-naming seemed shallow and at times even impertinent. He experienced it as an aggressive claiming of social territory. These reactions—sometimes negative—are not reasoned out. We simply have an impression based on our deep culture programming.

We can think of deep culture in terms of a "cultural onion" (see figure 2.2).[2] What we see on the surface hides deeper layers beneath. Surface behavior is interpreted through a filter of deep culture values, expectations, and assumptions. On the outside are visible manifestations of culture and social systems: food, buildings, ceremonies, and so on. Within a community, people share an understanding of what these things are and what they mean. When I see a church, school, or factory, I recognize it and know what it is for (whether I am in the habit of going inside or not).

Communities also share *norms*—expectations about how to do things. I know the type of behavior that is expected in churches and schools. Norms can be formalized (as in official rules and laws) or they can simply be expectations about

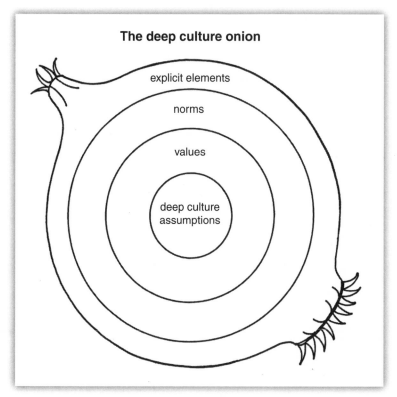

The deep culture onion

explicit elements

norms

values

deep culture assumptions

FIGURE 2.2   The deep culture onion

how things are done. Normally we shake with the right hand or dress up when going for a job interview. Norms are not always followed, of course. I may not wipe my feet or thank someone for their help or pay before leaving a restaurant. Yet not following norms doesn't mean that they're not still there. The challenge for cultural outsiders is ignorance of the ins and outs of these expectations. Something we might do without thinking in our own country (such as eating with the left hand) may create discomfort in another place (like parts of the Middle East).

If people are asked to explain norms, they may simply say that there's no reason in particular for them. We shake with the right hand "just because." At other times, however, they will answer by talking about *values*. Values tell us what's important when making choices about how to behave—how to be a good person. Japanese may tell you that people bow as a way to show respect, and that this leads to smooth human relations. And while some values are universal (it's good to care for your family), others aren't. Self-control is often seen as admirable in Ethiopia, while expressiveness is often valued in Brazil. And sometimes values come into conflict with each other. When my friend shows up wearing a new shirt that I don't like, should I tell him the truth (value directness) or pretend to like it (save face for my friend)?

While norms and values usually function out of everyday awareness, we can often, if called upon, explain them to some degree. Yet there is another layer of deep culture that lies beneath norms and values. It rests so deeply in our unconscious that even talking about it is a challenge. At the deepest level of our cultural onion lie hidden assumptions about reality—things which just *are*. The differing assumptions about hierarchy and deference found in Japan and in the United States are one example.

Deep culture assumptions can be talked about only as abstractions. They relate to fundamental elements of how we perceive reality. When stated as absolutes, they sound stark and extreme. Are men and women fundamentally similar or different? Is the physical world easily influenced by a spiritual or magical one? Is our first responsibility to ourselves as individuals or to the people around us? To what degree should we look to the past to guide our future actions? Are humans fundamentally selfish or evil? Should we trust rational thought over emotion and intuition?

This isn't meant as a list of philosophical questions that need to be debated. Most people recognize both intuitively and intellectually that none of these questions can be answered in absolute form. And individuals vary in how they think about these questions. Yet, there are powerful differences in deep cultural assumptions at work around the world. There is a level of acceptance of magic in many places in Africa that is out of place in Europe. Assumptions about gender differences vary starkly between Yemen and Finland. Chinese expectations about loyalty toward one's family may seem extreme in Canada but not in India. These assumptions are woven into the fabric that constitutes the world of everyday life. As deep culture learners, we seek to peel back these layers of meaning, both at home and abroad.

ASKING WHY

To investigate deeper layers of the cultural onion, we need to ask a series of "whys." What are the hidden meanings, assumptions, expectations, and values behind the way that people do things? If, for example, we ask, "Why are wedding dresses white?" we may be told, "It's simply a tradition" (a norm), or "Because white represents purity" (a value—it's good for brides to be pure).

Yet trying to ask questions about deeper hidden assumptions can provoke bewilderment or irritation. Try asking someone who grew up in Western Europe or the Americas, "Why is it good for a bride to be pure?" (figure 2.3). The question itself may seem impertinent. Yet there is a rich mix of deeply embedded cultural imagery still to be uncovered. For example, the traditional view of purity includes assumptions about good and evil and a human struggle

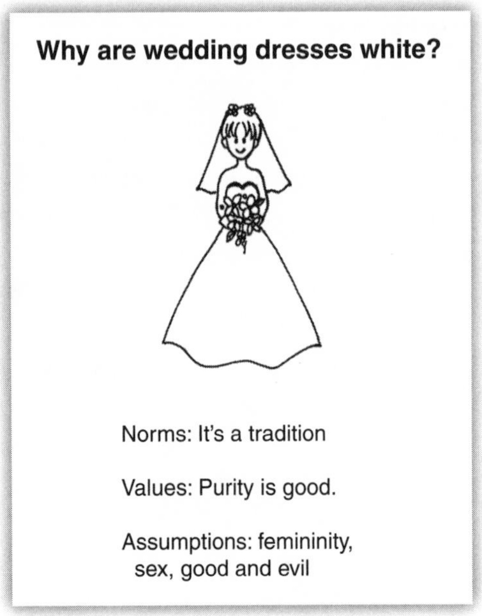

Why are wedding dresses white?

Norms: It's a tradition

Values: Purity is good.

Assumptions: femininity,
sex, good and evil

FIGURE 2.3   Why are wedding dresses white?

against a sinful, carnal nature. Regardless of whether you agree with these ideas as moral standards, people raised in the West will almost certainly understand the associations; we understand the implications in Christianity of Mary's virgin birth.

You may also provoke confusion (or consternation) by asking a Japanese, "Why is it important to show respect?" They could probably say something about the importance of smooth human relations, but would most likely have trouble articulating social assumptions about hierarchy. If they give it some thought, they may mention Confucius. Try asking an American, "Why do you think all humans are equal?" Or ask a Saudi, "Why is it important to be loyal to one's family?" These questions may seem like an attack. These are the questions that a deep culture traveler thinks about that are not easy (or polite) to discuss directly. Some things simply *are*.

As we'll see in chapter 4, the irritation you may provoke by questioning cultural assumptions is rooted directly in the hardware of our evolutionary biology. Threats to our beliefs and view of the world are experienced as threats to our person. Deep culture learners need to be ready to examine deeply held beliefs and values. It doesn't mean we have to give them up, but fully understanding them requires us to pull them up into the light and compare them with the views of people who think differently.

DEEP CULTURE AND INDIVIDUALITY

Some people object strongly to the idea that our behavior is powerfully influenced by such a vague phenomena as deep culture. After all, every human has different values, personalities, tastes, talents, experiences, living situations, and so on. Why so much focus on culture? One reason for this reaction is that people from Western Europe and its cultural cousins are socialized to focus on differences among individuals. The idea that one is different from others—a unique specimen—is of great importance for one's self-definition.

If you disagree that behavior is influenced by culture, remember that deep culture doesn't take away freedom of choice, nor does it make us any less individual. Instead, it provides the background against which we measure ourselves and give our actions meaning. In this sense, it functions like language. Each person uses his or her native language to express the richness of his or her individuality. No two people speak alike, and there are no purely "average" or "normal" speakers. Yet we share a linguistic framework that allows us to communicate smoothly in normal circumstances. We don't hear our "accent" until we go to another region.

The relationship between individuality and culture can be represented by a pyramid (see figure 2.4). At the base of the pyramid is a fundamental biology shared by humans everywhere. Our cultural programming is built on top of this as we are acculturated. In turn, we express our unique individuality through the lens of these deep cultural patterns. And as the dotted lines in figure 2.4 remind us, the separation between personal and cultural, cultural and universal, is often not clear.

Individuals from the same community have different experiences, opinions, personalities, and individual values. People vary greatly even within a single family. Yet this variation shouldn't blind us to our larger deep culture frameworks. For example, Americans may disagree whether

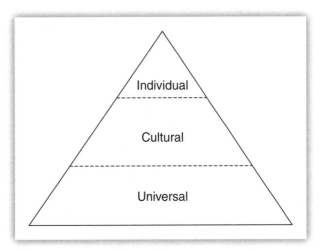

FIGURE 2.4　Individuality and culture

sex before marriage is immoral, but they share similar associations of the white wedding dress. They will also generally agree on other hidden cultural assumptions, such as the importance of the individual, a mistrust of hierarchy, the feeling that casual behavior is friendly, that humans are (or should be) in control of their own destiny, and so on. As an American, it was a shock to discover that my understanding of the world was so tied to American assumptions like these.

My emphasis on the unifying effects of culture goes against some current notions about the importance of cultural diversity. It's true that we participate not in a single "culture," but in countless communities from small to large. A cultural community can include groups as diverse as a family, a sports team, a social class, people who share ethnicity or language, and so on. And of course labels like American or Zimbabwean don't do justice to the tremendous diversity found within a country's borders. And some cultural communities are pan-national. In the end, however, we share many things with others in these broader communities; and the broadest commonalities are also frequently the deepest. It often requires a journey away to help us see larger cultural patterns. I never felt American until I left the United States. And I never felt like a Westerner until I lived in Asia. Strangely enough, moving to Europe felt like a homecoming even though I was a newcomer there.

Where I am from, attempts at self-understanding are often centered on trying to understand what's special or distinct within us. We're told to pursue our dreams and uncover our hidden talents—the individual is celebrated. This can enrich us by helping us take control of our lives and discover our particular talents. Yet my sojourns have shown me that there is another way to learn about ourselves. By understanding ourselves as cultural beings, shaped by the world we grew up in, we can add another dimension to our self-understanding.

We often make unconscious choices without realizing that there are other options. Perhaps we should say that the communities we live in have made a series of choices that we have adopted unknowingly. It can be a useful lesson in humility to see that so many of our choices are influenced in this way. This doesn't mean that we're not unique, but it does imply that we have some work to do. This is the work of deep culture learning. By uncovering deep culture patterns, new choices—perhaps even new worlds—can open up to us. And this will ultimately enrich us as the unique individuals that we are.

CHAPTER THREE

Deep Culture
as a
Concept

I LIVED ABROAD FOR MANY YEARS before finding out that culture, and cultural difference, could be studied more formally. I first discovered this when I came across a book by Edward Hall, an anthropologist who is considered to be the father of the study of intercultural communication. I then took workshops and courses, did graduate study, and eventually wrote textbooks on intercultural communication.

Throughout this process of academic learning, I have struggled with the slipperiness of the whole concept of culture. It can be stated so broadly as to be nearly meaningless—when, for example, we define culture simply as the shared attributes of a group. My interest is, more narrowly, the unconscious patterns of culture that we become aware of during intercultural experiences—that is, deep culture. Deep culture seems to me to be at the core of understanding intercultural experiences.

Yet even this more narrow way of looking at culture can be difficult to pin down. So in this chapter I take a closer look at deep culture as a concept—as an idea that can be argued over in explicit terms. This can help us grasp it more fully and understand how it can be studied scientifically. After looking at this more formal view of deep culture, we discuss why understanding deep culture as a concept doesn't always help us see its influences in our own lives.

IN THE BRAIN AND IN THE AIR

Let's first look at how we acquire deep culture. I've talked about deep culture as a kind of mental programming. As we grow up, we integrate cultural patterns that we find in our environment. In that sense, deep culture is not only in our brains, it's "in the air"—or in the patterns of behavior and thinking of people around us. An important element of deep culture is linguistic knowledge and the worldview that goes along with it. The associations of "wedding" that I have as an American come from a combination of the general associations of that word (a white dress, and so on) and my own personal experiences with weddings.

Deep culture patterns include many other elements as well. A child growing up in a rural community in Senegal acquires a different sense of time—and therefore experiences time differently—than someone growing up in Switzerland. Patterns related to the expression of emotion, assumptions about hierarchy, use of personal space, and taboo subjects and objects are somehow absorbed in the process of experiencing life in one's home community.

Deep culture operates as networks of meaning in our brains. But it is also evident at the macro level—or perhaps we should say the meta-level—and reflected in the social practices of our community. To study deep culture empirically, it's not enough to look either inside ourselves or at the functioning of the brain. We have to look at patterns of interaction among people in cultural communities. To see why this is so, I suggest you visit your neighborhood park and try the following experiment.

First, look around until you find some ants. Put some crumbled bits of cookie nearby. Come back later, and you will see that a line of ants has formed to carry the food back to the colony. If you try this several times, you will see that the more food that you put down, the greater the number of ants will be working at taking it back. If you block the line of ants by dropping a stone in its path, you'll see that although at first this throws the ants into confusion, after a few minutes they form a new trail around the stone, always using the shortest route possible. Yet how is it possible for ants to make the decisions necessary for these behaviors? Who decides how many ants should be sent to pick up the food? How do ants know which path around the stone is the shortest?

DEEP CULTURE AS AN EMERGENT PROPERTY

Of course, there is no command-and-control structure in an ant colony. Instead, the intelligence of an ant colony is the product of the interaction among the ants. It is an *emergent property*—a complex whole that emerges out of the interaction of simpler parts. Each ant operates under a simple set of guidelines it uses to choose its behaviors—finding food, carrying it back to the nest, and so on. For example, when given the choice between two pheromone trails (chemical signals used to communicate), ants follow the stronger one. So although individual ants will randomly attempt to get around the stone dropped in their path, those that happen to follow the shortest route to the path they were looking for will find it more quickly, laying down pheromone as they go. Other ants follow this signal, and the pheromone on the shortest path is reinforced. The programming of each ant is quite simple, yet when all the ants work together, they create behaviors that exhibit larger patterns, or intelligences. This *group intelligence* (see figure 3.1) is a product of many simple interactions which combine in complex ways.[1]

In the same way, deep culture is created and maintained by the interaction of individuals. We make individual decisions within the framework of the worldview we've been imprinted with as we've grown up. And just as it would be hard for an ant to see the larger patterns of the colony, it is hard for us to see the hidden guidelines that shape our thinking. An ant would have to notice hidden

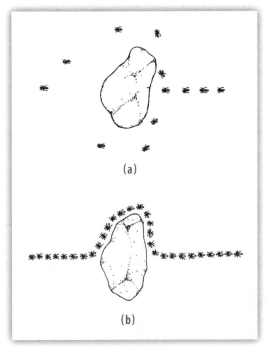

(a)

(b)

FIGURE 3.1   Group intelligence

patterns (finding the shortest route) and extrapolate about how those patterns work. The ant could then see that its internal programming—the rules or intuitions it has about when and how to lay down pheromone—connects it to the larger purpose and movement of the colony.

We too must search out hidden patterns in our behavior and thinking. When I lived in Mexico, I found that my male Mexican friends often came farther into my personal space than did my friends in the United States. In Japan, I found the opposite. By making these comparisons, I started to indentify within myself the general parameters of how space is used in U.S. American culture. But this required an extrapolation from many individual interactions. Just as ants are continually exchanging information with each other, so we too perpetuate and contribute to the larger patterns in our communities. An awareness of these patterns requires an ongoing commitment to deciphering the interactions of everyday life in different places.

DEEP CULTURE AS THE "RULES OF THE GAME"

Humans obviously have more awareness of their interactions and choices than ants. Yet they are broadly defined by community standards. You may feel, for example, that you choose whether to be liberal or conservative. But the dichotomy of "liberal" as opposed to "conservative" is part of the language and thinking of your community. You can choose to associate with either, both, or neither of those labels, yet the labels themselves persist and evolve through ongoing use. The shared meanings of deep culture are bigger and more persistent than any individual choice that we make.

In that sense, deep culture can be thought of as the "rules of the game." The "rules" are the frameworks we use to think about our lives and the standards that are expected from us when we interact with others. Each individual plays the game in his own way, but the "game" itself is shared at the group level. The deep culture learner tries to uncover these hidden rules.

Let's try a more concrete parallel example in our search for conceptual insight into deep culture. We all know that the game of soccer exists. But where is soccer? Mostly, soccer exists as an understanding of the game within the heads of the players and fans, as well as in the patterns found in the playing of the game itself (think of an aerial view of a game). The things used to play soccer—the goal, the ball, the rule book—are not soccer per se; they are the objects that soccer players utilize in order to carry out the game they've agreed to play. In the same way, deep culture exists as shared understandings. The objects that a community makes—churches, temples, buildings, artwork, history books and so on—are like the soccer ball. They are things that have an agreed-upon meaning within the game of society and human interaction (see figure 3.2).

Often, of course, the rules we play by are unspoken. Soccer has official rules that determine the formal parameters of the game, but there are also assumptions about what constitutes fair play, an acceptable level of aggression, the importance of teamwork, and so on. And so too does each community have explicit laws, rules, regulations, and also hidden assumptions and expectations about how people are expected to conduct themselves—what's reasonable and fair, how to form relationships, and an infinite number of informal rules of the game.

Each person contributes her own understanding of deep culture to the larger group. This ongoing exchange makes

FIGURE 3.2   Deep culture as the "rules of the game"

culture dynamic. Deep culture patterns evolve with the times, as we can often see when a senior citizen attempts to communicate with a teenager. Yet at the deepest levels, these patterns change only very slowly, which is why we can find historical continuity to deep culture over periods of thousands of years. The rationality of the Greeks lives on in Europeans, pre-Columbian attitudes toward death live on in Mexico, and many observations Alexis de Tocqueville made about Americans remain valid 150 years later.

WHAT SPECIALISTS HAVE TO SAY

Trying to gaining a broad scientific understanding of deep culture can be frustrating. Both the inner (our brains) and outer (our societies) sides of deep culture have been studied in different forms by a wide range of specialists, but deep culture is such a broad, pervasive phenomena that it must be broken into much smaller pieces to study systematically. It's hard to study as a whole.

Yet the work of a wide range of specialists can teach us a lot. Cognitive psychologists study the *cognitive unconscious*, the parts of the brain responsible for automatic processing and making sense of perceptual data.[2] Intercultural communication specialists, sociologists, social psychologists, and anthropologists study social systems, institutions, and artistic output of cultural communities. Linguists study the connection between language and culture. Some economists study how deep culture values effect economic development.[3] Philosophers and religious scholars study cosmologies that evolve in conjunction with deep culture.

Deep culture values and communication styles are widely studied in international business because cultural misunderstanding is expensive.[4] Even some advertisers use research related to deep culture in order to better influence consumer's choices.[5] One study, for example, found that people who were bicultural and bilingual responded differently to the same advertisement depending on which language they were asked about it in. This showed that they were activating different *schema*—mental maps—to make sense of what they were seeing.[6]

Of course we can't be experts in all these areas. But we should be able to test our understanding of deep culture against the theories and conclusions of different fields of scientific study. Despite my frequent reference to the importance of personal experience and cultural self-awareness, I believe we shouldn't shy away from an attempt at rigorous empirical inquiry.

DEEP CULTURE LEARNING

While it has been useful for me to pursue a scientific understanding of deep culture, I admit that my interest in this topic is more personal. Attempting to understand deep culture has helped me grow as a human being. When I first lived abroad in Mexico, for example, I kept finding that what I thought of as "the world" was actually the world as seen by U.S. Americans. What was normal for me was not normal for the Mexicans I met and befriended. My Mexican girlfriend at the time complained that she could never predict when I would be upset at her for being late to meet me. She found me both rigid and capricious. She would surprise me, for example, by being offended when I didn't position myself on the street side of the sidewalk while walking together. "Are you trying to sell me?" she said more than once. And while sometimes these discoveries were frustrating, for the most part I felt liberated because the patterns underlying these confusions eventually started to become more obvious.

Unfortunately, unmasking deep culture's influence on us is difficult. It's not threatening to learn about deep culture in a theoretical way, as scholars do. But directly experiencing the influence of deep culture in our own lives can be stressful. Most fundamentally, adapting to new places can tax our tolerance and flexibility. Particularly in the age of globalization, we can isolate ourselves in a cocoon of familiarity even when we are abroad. It's often not that difficult to become fairly comfortable in a new environment—to find our niche as a tourist, traveler, or expatriate. What's hard is to not stop there—to seek out a challenging degree of adaptation and join more fully in the communities that we have contact with.

At home, deep culture is kept invisible by the routines that give continuity to our lives—routines of perception and behavior. Every time you shop at local store you rely on deep culture routines (for example, "Will that be cash or charge?"). When you eat the same breakfast for years on end, when you greet your colleagues without thinking, or when you spout opinions that you heard on TV, you are perpetuating the influence of deep culture in your life. To pursue deep culture learning at home requires an awareness of how often we function using our cultural and personal autopilot.

Breaking even the smallest routine engages our ability to learn new cultural patterns. It also helps if you are nonjudgmental, empathetic, unafraid of making mistakes, curious, comfortable with ambiguity, and willing to take a trial-and-error approach to new experiences. In theory, we don't have to leave home at all to discover deep culture (sociologists and social psychologists, for example, often study it systematically). But there's nothing like going abroad and trying to fit into the daily life of a different community to bring it into focus.

LOOKING INSIDE OURSELVES

To understand why it's difficult to become aware of our own deep culture programming, let's imagine someone—let's call him Bob (see figure 3.3). Bob lives his life largely as the people around him expect. To ease social interaction, Bob regularly speaks in platitudes. He, for the most part, accepts the conventions he has learned growing up—though he considers himself a bit of a rebel in certain areas. When Bob's view of the world is threatened, he gets bothered or indignant. When Bob travels to foreign lands, he tends to

FIGURE 3.3   Bob

judge people based on standards from back home. Sometimes, though, Bob simply doesn't notice the differences he
encounters, finding instead that "people are just people."

We may find Bob dull, but he feels himself to be reasonable and original. Bob feels attached to his choices. He has
political and moral convictions. He feels himself unique
because he sees people around him who disagree with him
on these issues. But most of Bob's opinions are ideas that he
has picked up from those around him. They represent part
of a dialogue that Bob's community is having with itself.
When he watches the news from foreign countries, he is
struck by the differences in what is reported.

Bob also feels original because he has his own personality. He tends to be, let's say, friendly and outgoing. But Bob
expresses his friendliness in much the same way that others
in his community do. The particular combination of traits
that make up Bob's personality is very original, but the way

that these qualities are expressed follows a predictable pattern. Bob doesn't notice this, though, because he's caught up in being himself. And he doesn't notice he's caught up in being himself because he's never gotten to know people who have a fundamentally different sense of these things. If Bob decides to travel or live abroad, especially if his journey involves using a different language, he'll need to make some big adjustments. Although we describe this process as cultural learning, for Bob it's also a deeply personal challenge. Even the simplest adjustments to life abroad, such as eating new food, can be discomforting. Bigger challenges may render Bob intolerant and judgmental. He is likely to easily accept cultural difference that reinforces his sense of personal self-importance (like the strong emphasis on hospitality in some places), but he is likely to resist cultural difference that calls his view of the world into question. He will judge people based on standards from back home yet feel confident that he is simply reporting the facts. He will simply "know" that people in country X tend to be pushy, dishonest, or underdeveloped. Once these ethnocentric assumptions are reinforced by his lived experience, he will say, "I know because I've been there!"

WE ARE ALL BOB

Living abroad forced me to accept that I am more like Bob than I might like to admit—I think we all are. That's not a failure on our part, it's how we humans are built—it's a product of our evolutionary psychology. We evolved as social primates who live in groups and adapt to our environment by creating a collective view of the world that is perpetuated and defended. This ability has allowed us to inhabit (some would say overrun) nearly every environmental niche on the planet.

Now, however, we are more frequently rubbing up against difference. We travel, live abroad, or spend our days in multicultural workplaces, yet our parochial tendencies remain. For all the information and images we have of the larger world, our everyday lives are largely shaped by the expectations and views of those nearby. We haven't changed all that much. Globalization has certainly not brought an end to prejudice, misunderstanding, or war. In many cases it has exacerbated it. Living abroad and learning foreign languages is still not easy. We're mostly as ethnocentric as we've always been, even if the trappings of our everyday lives are more connected and cosmopolitan.

So how can we become aware of deep culture in our lives? Being open to the cultural diversity that already exists in our community is a good starting point. Yet I also believe we gain a lot by leaving the comforts of home. Remember that globalization has made it easier to insulate ourselves from deep cultural difference. We can comfort ourselves with pizza, read our local newspaper online, drink our favorite beer, and spend time with the foreigners (same age, same hobbies, same profession) who are the most like us.

But what a waste! For the first time in history, millions of people have the chance to explore the deepest roots of the human experience—to go beyond the habits of the local tribe. To understand the diversity of the human "tribe" today, I suggest we take a journey back in time, to an era when humans had bodies and brains like we do but hadn't developed culture, community, and identity as we know it today. If we can walk in their footsteps, we may gain a deeper undestanding of ourselves.

CHAPTER FOUR

The Evolution
of
Deep Culture

L AST YEAR I SPENT A WEEK in the Daintree tropical rainforest in Australia. While there, I was struck by my ignorance. I couldn't tell one plant from another and would have been absolutely helpless if I had gotten lost. Yet people have lived in similar environments for tens of thousands of years, gained intimate knowledge of their environment, and developed lifestyles, beliefs, and values adapted to life in those places. Could I ever understand the experiences, wisdom, and insights of such people?

Likewise, while living in Mexico I visited isolated indigenous communities deep in the mountains of the Sierra Madre Occidental, where I witnessed ceremonies with roots in religious traditions going back more than 500 years. There was hypnotic dancing around a fire, offerings of tobacco and chanting. These Mesoamerican traditions were so different from anything that I as a U.S. American knew that I found myself wondering if I could ever fully understand them. And yet, if I had grown up in a rainforest or in a Toltec village in Mesoamerica, these traditions and beliefs would have been as normal to me as Starbucks and computers are to me now.

This raises a fundamental question facing deep culture travelers: What is our capacity for understanding people whose lives are very different from our own? We are all human, after all. Yet the variety of human experience is staggering. In the history of our species, the ways of life that have been considered normal by one people or another have varied beyond imagination. From the arctic to the deserts, from cannibalism to vegetarianism, from cattle raiding to pyramid building—slaves and royalty, shamans and rocket science, zombies and Mickey Mouse—it's all been normal to someone at one time and place or another.

An important first step of cultural learning is the simple recognition of just how different cultural worlds can be. Try to imagine, for example, what kind of person you would be had you grown up in a different country, speaking a different language. Developing a deep appreciation of other cultural realities often requires years of exposure. Even after five years of living in Japan and studying Japanese, I felt that I was just starting to get the hang of honorific language and the Japanese sense for how best to manage human relations.

Truly understanding the human experience requires tremendous imaginative empathy. We need to attempt to get "in the heads" of people whose experience of the world is very different from our own. To practice this, let us travel back in time and try to understand the life experiences of Stone Age humans—bands of hunter-gatherers with bodies and brain capacities that were fundamentally the same as ours, living tens of thousands of years ago. Perhaps this exercise can shed light on how culture came to be a defining element of the human experience.

THE EVOLUTION OF DEEP CULTURE

The human brain achieved its current form perhaps 250,000 years ago.[1] Yet the first anatomically modern humans didn't behave and interact as we do. Their cultural evolution was—by today's standards at least—agonizingly slow. For example, once an advance was made in the technology of stone tools, it spread without variation and remained stable across vast distances for tens of thousands of years. Imagine 500 generations living in the same way, using the same stone tools, without apparent innovation or expression of community identity. You made your stone cutter in the same way as others had for millennia (see figure 4.1).

The experience of life at this time must have been quite different from what humans experience now. We lived in groups, communicated with each other to some degree, and learned from each other, but it seems that culture was rudimentary. It's not clear that different groups looked at the world in distinct ways. Were there different beliefs and

FIGURE 4.1   Bifacial points, engraved ochre, and bone
tools from 75,000 to 80,000 years ago

traditions that guided behavior? Were individuals aware of themselves as members of a unique community? Did people look to the future and past, or did they live more or less in the present of immediate experience? The latter may be more likely, since communities seemed to acquire hardly any new knowledge over time. Perhaps the limiting factor was communication. A lack of fully developed language may have prevented people from sharing experiences and developing new technology.

About 50,000 years ago, however, there was a sudden shift referred to as the *Paleolithic revolution*, or the "big bang of consciousness." Human behavior began to evolve much more quickly.

People started paying attention to burying the dead. They developed sophisticated hunting techniques, started wearing clothes, and began painting caves. For the first time in history, human communities that lived in different places showed variation at the local level. The buttons or fish hooks (see figure 4.2) of my community were different from those on the other side of the mountain.

What caused this shift and precisely how quickly it happened is not clear. It may have been related to the development of language. It's possible that a genetic variation that improved some key cognitive capacity swept through human populations. In any case, we can say that since at least 50,000 years ago humans have communicated with each other and made sense of the world using mental processes very similar to the ones people use today.

It's likely that deep culture—the existence of a shared worldview, values, and community standards—dates at least to this time. I imagine that it also corresponds with the human ability to identify an "us" based on those who share not only physical things like territory but a way of commu-

FIGURE 4.2   Neolithic fish hook

nicating and explaining things. As humans gained the ability to speak and think abstractly, we were better able to collaborate and share information. This led to a reinforcing cycle of more complex behaviors, technologies, and social organization.

As part of this process, we gained the ability to imagine future events, tell stories, and find personal ways to explain life's important events (birth, death, rivalry, natural phenomena, and so on). We started to live in an increasingly conceptual world and gained the ability to be physically present but mentally somewhere else. We started to live in our heads as much as in our bodies. This was a monumental step. It was, in a very literal sense, a leap of consciousness.

It's difficult to say precisely what relationship there is between the ability to live in a symbolic world of culture and the development of consciousness. At some point, however, the mental world humans live in came to involve both meaning shared at the community level (language and worldview) and the personal awareness of oneself as an actor in our perceptual world.

Human consciousness is not a singular thing. We have a base consciousness of wakefulness, a state that alternates between sleep and periods of engaged attention. Animals are also conscious in this sense. But human consciousness includes a sense of oneself as being apart from one's environment—an actor in a world of meaningful action.

And it involves the sense that one can observe the self in the act of experiencing the world. So not only are we aware of ourselves as actors, we are aware of the fact that we are aware. These capacities are just now starting to be more fully understood.[2]

And what is this "world of meaningful action" that we perceive? It's not just the world of physical objects like trees, mountains, and tigers. Objects have meaning; they are associated with memories and ideas. We pay great attention to other people, recognizing them as having experiential existence like ours. We know that other people have individualized worlds in their heads, just as we do in ours. Often when we talk about the world, we fail to make the distinction between the world of physical objects (which your cat is also aware of) and the conceptual world of symbols and meaning (which your cat doesn't share with you).[3]

Think of how little time you spend in an average day paying active attention to your physical environment. If you work in an office, you may spend hours on end in a tiny monotonous space, yet as you talk on the phone, analyze problems, set conscious goals, and decide on lunch plans, you have the sense of participating in the "real world." The real world of human beings is primarily a conceptual one. And our brain is so proficient at constructing reality independent of external stimuli that our dreams at night can take on the qualities of epic journeys to wonderful and terrifying places.

Our evolutionary ancestors lived in a conceptual world that allowed for an explosion of creativity that vastly changed human communities. But let's not forget that our present conceptual world is still tied to our primate past. Watch a troop of chimpanzees and it's easy to recognize elements of our shared evolutionary roots such as territoriality, a social nature, hierarchy, and reciprocity. But humans are different from chimpanzees in an important respect. Our territory corresponds not just to a physical space, but to a mental one as well. We may feel threatened when someone attacks our ideas. Our mental world is as often as real and important to us as the physical world. Chimpanzees affiliate with kin and others in their troop. Humans do this, but we also affiliate based on adherence to shared ideals, beliefs, and polities. Chimpanzees may seek favor by grooming or sharing food, while humans may do so by agreeing with what other people think and say. Chimpanzees physically signal submission to a higher-ranking member of the troop. Our dominance and submission is also encoded in types of language and dress. Have you ever felt irritated when someone neglects to say "thank you" for a gift? In the conceptual world of human societies, phrases like this are expected at certain times and places. But it is our primal need to feel that favors are reciprocated that gives rise to our irritation.

Understanding the architecture of deep culture and human consciousness can help us better comprehend the experience of rainforest dwellers, pre-Columbian Mesoamericans, or any cultural community. We can be certain that every human community during the past 50,000 years lived in a rich world of meaning and symbolism. Regardless of the environment—island, desert, or grassy plain—humans create meaning about what is around them. A tree may be a sacred being or a building material. A color can mean anything we decide it does. And when we are surrounded by others who share our meanings, we form strong bonds with them. From this, deep culture explorers learn that a key to understanding different communities is to enter into the symbolic world that they create for themselves. To know people, you have to understand how they think. You have to get into their heads.

DEEP CULTURE AND
SOCIAL ORGANIZATION

The "big bang of consciousness" that occurred 50,000 years ago was not the only monumental event in human cultural history. Up until 10,000 years ago, humans never lived in groups larger than about 150 people. For more than 200,000 years we lived exclusively as hunters and gatherers; we owned only what we could carry and followed the resources we needed to survive. Then, 10,000 to 15,000 years ago, humans started to settle down. We developed agriculture, domesticated animals, and created larger settlements.

Living in larger groups (think villages and kingdoms as opposed to small bands), humans were required to learn to collaborate to an unprecedented degree. We had to develop codes of conduct that allowed us to interact with people who belonged to our community but whom we didn't know. Some believe that genetic changes also made people correspondingly less aggressive.[4] In any case, living in larger groups sped up the creative explosion of cultural evolution. Successful technologies spread; groups that developed social cohesion were able to outcompete those who didn't. Cosmologies were elaborated, social systems were created, value systems were developed and passed on. This process proceeded so quickly that a mere 5,000 years after beginning to live in settled communities, humans developed expansive empires, writing systems, and an unprecedented level of social complexity.

This evolution is often talked about in terms of *memes*, a unit of cultural information, such as an idea, practice, or symbol, that people learn from each other and that can spread throughout a community and evolve over time.[5] A meme can be nearly anything that we learn: a melody, an understanding of a new technology, a religious belief, or a ceremony. Taken together, a community's memes represent the sum total of its shared knowledge. I believe that some very important memes are often unconscious, internalized as values and assumptions about the nature of the world. The memes that helped economic production and social cohesion gave competitive advantages to the communities that developed them.

It may sound as though all of this cultural history lies deep in the past. But the hospitality of Arab communities today has roots in social practices developed over millennia in the desert, just as the communal values of Asians developed in the context of the collaborative task of growing rice. The social worlds that deep culture travelers find when they travel to new places are the product of thousands of years of evolutionary development. And they are still firmly connected to the drives and intuitions that we share with our primate cousins.

Through much of our evolutionary history, humans have lived in small bands, collaborating against outsiders, defending territory, and competing for resources. In that sense, the increasing complexity of human social organization has created a unique challenge. We increasingly come into contact with people who are different than we are, but cognitively and biologically we maintain a strong tendency toward the ethnocentrism of our ancestors. (Ethnocentrism is the natural tendency to see one's own culture as primary.) Our evolutionary biology has not designed us to intuitively understand cultural difference or easily collaborate with those we don't know.

We've been slow to discover this. It's been only in the past 200 years or so that people have started the systematic study of culture, cultural difference, and our evolution as social primates. Formal attempts to understand the unconscious mind were very limited before the beginning of the twentieth century. The particular challenges of communicating and working across cultural boundaries, as well as an increased understanding of how intercultural experiences can affect us psychologically, have begun to be examined only in the second half of the twentieth century.

Fortunately, all in all we have learned a lot. In the next chapter, we'll visit with some of the people who have contributed greatly to our current knowledge about deep culture and the intercultural experience. This will get us ready to begin our own journeys of deep culture exploration.

CHAPTER FIVE

The Discovery
of
Deep Culture

THE YEAR WAS 1883. Franz Boas was exhausted, freezing cold, and famished. He knew that he was at risk of dying in a harsh landscape of ice and snow. He had been sledding for twenty-six hours through the Arctic with temperatures at times below 46°C. He and his companions had gotten lost. Most probably, he had underestimated the challenge he had set for himself—to live in and study Inuit communities. Yet his confidence is understandable. He was an accomplished man back in Germany—a scientist with a doctorate in physics.

Yet now he was helpless and lost. His miscalculation had put him at grave risk. Yet finally, to their great relief, Franz and his companions found shelter with an Inuit community. They were shown hospitality and allowed to warm up and rest. It had been a harrowing experience that affected Franz deeply. The following day, he reflected on his increasing appreciation for his own ignorance. Despite Franz's education and capability back home, in Inuit communities in the Arctic he was helpless. He was forced to depend absolutely on his hosts for directions, food, and companionship. He was in their world.

This experience was a formative one. When he went back to Europe, Franz Boas (see figure 5.1) published a book about his experiences and became a leading expert in the study of culture.[1] Eventually he moved to the United States, where he started the first doctoral program in anthropology, becoming, in effect, the father of modern anthropology in the United States. His insights contributed to a broad rethinking of how culture shapes human behavior.[2]

In Franz's time, it was typically believed that culture evolved from simple to more complex. Thus, a community living in small groups in the jungle with few possessions was considered less developed than, say, a nation state or empire. But Franz came to think that the essence of the human experience is not technical (the tools that we use), but mental. What most clearly distinguishes one community from another is the patterns of meaning that each community shares—what they believe about the world and what they expect of the people around them. Franz's experiences in the Arctic helped him experience the world of meaning that the Inuit live in—one as rich and complex as the one he knew in Germany.

FIGURE 5.1   Franz Boas

Franz's insights did not come easily. He had, at the time, the rare opportunity to engage deeply with a radically different way of living and seeing the world. He also had the right mix of curiosity and openness to avoid exoticizing or looking down on the people he met. And he was able to consciously examine his experiences to try to answer some of the deeper questions about the human experience. Franz's journey was intellectual but also experiential. The whole-body experience of living life as others live it helped Franz's perception shift in fundamental ways. He started as an outsider and slowly learned to peer into the world as experienced by Inuit communities. He was helped by a neutral stance (he didn't feel himself superior to his hosts) and a penchant for thoughtful analysis.

I believe that this neutral stance of thoughtful analysis can help us set aside some of our own deep culture biases. And intellectual knowledge that is gained through formal study can help us make better sense of our lived experience. So I'd like to take a journey of imaginative empathy—we'll try to put ourselves into the minds of Franz's contemporaries. We'll then trace some of the intellectual insights gained about culture during the past 100 years.

CULTURE IN AN AGE OF "PROGRESS"

Imagine a visit to the Exposition Universelle (World's Fair) in Paris of 1900. It was a remarkable event. Fifty million people visited more than 76,000 exhibits. The fair showcased a century's worth of scientific and industrial accomplishments. The crowning glory was the Eiffel Tower (built in 1889), an engineering tour de force that transformed iron girders and steel cables into a symbol of the beauty of industrial progress.

If we had attended the fair, we would have seen escalators, movies with sound, electric turbines, and Campbell's Soup (the gold medal from this fair still decorates the cans

FIGURE 5.2   Eiffel Tower, Exposition Universelle (World's Fair), Paris 1900

today). The whole spectacle was designed to highlight the breathtaking industrial and scientific accomplishments of the previous century. The nineteenth century had seen kings and feudal Europe replaced by nation states and global trading empires. The turn of the twentieth century was a confident time.

Yet the Paris exhibit included, among its symbols of "progress," a human zoo. People were brought from faraway places and displayed along with artifacts found in the daily lives of "primitive peoples." The people exhibited were believed by many to be at a stage of evolutionary development somewhere between apes and Europeans. This was not uncommon in Europe and the United States at the time. The photo in figure 5.3, from an exhibit in the Bronx Zoo in New York, shows Ota Benga, a Congolese Pygmy brought to

FIGURE 5.3   Ota Benga, Bronx Zoo, 1906

the United States in 1904. Ota Benga "worked" in different exhibits and lived at the Bronx Zoo.

Even in 1900 there were, of course, people who found such treatment offensive or inhuman. Yet the fundamental idea behind these exhibits—that "primitive" peoples were less evolved than people from Europe and the United States—was relatively common. Part of this was due to simple ignorance. Almost no one had firsthand knowledge of such different cultural communities. What people did hear came from explorers and adventurers who often popularized and sensationalized these communities. Rather than judge this ignorance, we should wonder how we ourselves would have experienced these things had we been raised in Europe or the United States in the late nineteenth century. Fortunately, although ethnocentrism, racism, and prejudice are alive and well in our time, we have come a long way since then in our understanding of differences among peoples. Franz Boas' work was part of a great intellectual shift. Even in 1900, things were changing fast. New transportation technology made it easier to visit far-off lands. Increasingly, people like Boas set off in the spirit of scientific exploration to study "the natives" in indigenous settings. And many of these scientists made a startling discovery—though perhaps not the one they expected. These cultural explorers found that, by immersing themselves in faraway communities, their view of the world was gradually yet profoundly transformed.

The intellectual certainty that marked the late nineteenth century was soon swept away. By the early 1930s, Newtonian physics was obsolete, the political order in Europe had been broken by a world war, modern art had challenged received wisdom about beauty, a great depression had halted economic development worldwide, and modern composers and jazz had reshaped musical sensibilities.

When you immerse yourself deeply into a new community, the worldview you find there can envelop you in a new sense of what's normal and natural. You start to value things differently, take on new social roles, and so on. When you go home, you experience a state of reverse culture shock in which your view of your original home is transformed even though nothing has changed there. The original goal of cultural explorers like Franz Boas was an objective scientific description of life in other places, but they started to see that this goal of objectiveness was built on cultural assumptions. As Franz Boas found out, objectivity was elusive. One could describe the world as seen by "the natives" or as seen by people back home, but neither view is more advanced, meaningful, or necessarily objective.

These insights led anthropologists to reconsider the idea that the people they studied were primitive. It became clear that the internal lives of the people studied were as deep and sophisticated as those of supposedly civilized people. Their priorities and view of life were simply different. Who could say what progress was? Normal was in the eye of the beholder.

These experiences also gave these explorers a fresh perspective on their own societies. They found many things of value in the "exotic" customs of other places and shared their insights when they returned home.

At times this led to heated debate. For example, in 1928, Margaret Mead published *The Coming of Age in Samoa*, a best-selling account of the life of adolescents in Polynesia.[3] The book provoked controversy in the United States because it argued that what Americans considered to be universal stages of development were in fact cultural conventions. Mead insisted that adolescent rebellion and sexual taboos were not biological but were norms learned unconsciously from our community. She and other anthropologists argued that studying life in faraway places illuminates hidden aspects of our own cultural values and provides the means to improve our own society.

More recently, Mead's understanding of Polynesian culture has been called into question. There are doubts about her ability to understand the local language and suspicion that she may have been misled by her informants. She may have had preconceived ideas that she wanted validated. As we've seen, it's not easy to enter another cultural community, understand how things work, and make valid comparisons with the world we come from. In addition, research in evolutionary psychology has made it clear that humans are not simply general purpose learning machines that can be totally shaped by culture. Regardless of the limitations of Mead's conclusions, however, the larger lesson from what she attempted is that life abroad has something to teach us about life at home. Learning about others teaches us about ourselves.

Also in the early twentieth century, linguistic anthropologists were exploring the relationship between language and perception. Some argued that language is not simply a set of labels that are affixed to an unchanging world, and that people who speak different languages live in different perceptual worlds. It's not so much that language affects our perception of physical reality (though some researchers have found a bit of evidence for this), but that language represents the symbolic world of a community, as it explains its own experiences *to itself.*[4]

To be raised speaking a particular language is to experience a social reality that can be accurately described only using that language. The *freedom* known to Americans is not the same as the *liberté* known in France or *jiyu* in Japanese. After two years in Japan I had an intense "Aha!" moment when, at a party, I got an intuitive feel for the word *nakama.* *Nakama* is a nearly untranslatable word that describes a feeling of friendship or connection to those with whom we share a group-centered relationship.

Translation is always approximate; words exist in relation to other words and to the ideas that describe the world within a community of speakers. *Freedom* in the United States has connotations of individual choice and self-determination. *Liberté* has rich associations with the ideals and assumptions of the French Revolution. Some research has shown that people who are raised biculturally access different networks of meaning when switching languages, while non-bicultural bilinguals have, to some degree, simply pasted the new language onto their existing view of the world.[5]

These insights about language as a set of labels for a subjective cultural worldview dovetail with insights by constructivist philosophers and educators such as Jean Piaget. Piaget showed that our understanding of reality is constructed by our minds; it's not just a mechanical process of registering the qualities of an objective physical world around us. Piaget showed, among other things, that children's learning progresses as their brains become capable of processing information in more sophisticated ways. They weren't simply learning what *is* but were gaining the ability to construct a more sophisticated view of the world.

THE UNCONSCIOUS

As the first anthropologists were experimenting with the mind-bending task of living in new cultural worlds (a kind of outside-in approach to self-understanding), others were looking at the mind from the inside out. In the early 1900s, Sigmund Freud, Carl Jung, and others were trying to understand the cognitive and emotional processes that take place outside of conscious awareness. Their work has been so influential that today it can be difficult to imagine why their descriptions of the unconscious were considered so revolutionary. At the time, the notion that we weren't aware of our own mental processes was fascinating (and a bit threatening).

These days the work of trying to understand the unconscious mind has expanded from the field of psychology to the world of neurology and cognitive science. Freud's view of a rational mind controlling powerful emotions and desires has been supplemented by an understanding of the how the brain processes information unconsciously. We've also started to see that our impulses and desires are closely tied with our evolutionary biology.

For sojourners, an understanding of how the unconscious mind works can be a powerful tool of cultural learning. Reflecting on intercultural experiences has some things in common with the introspection practiced in psychotherapy. Both include a desire to identify hidden patterns of thought and feelings. Both can involve a reevaluation of our priorities and values. Yet cultural learners are more focused on discovering how their internal processes fit into the context of their cultural community. For me to understand Mexico, I had to reflect on my Americanness. Living in France after having spent years in Asia brought to light elements of my cultural self that I shared with the French (as a Westerner) and those that were different (as an American).

EDWARD HALL AND INTERCULTURAL COMMUNICATION

In 1959, *The Silent Language* was published by Edward Hall. Hall was the first person to systematically study out-of-awareness cultural differences and use the term *intercultural communication*. He was a visionary whose fundamental premise was that humankind needs to break free of cultural conditioning. He spoke of culture catching people in a web of delusions, one of which is that life makes sense and that we are sane. According to Hall, culture traps us in a series of attachments wherein we defend and protect ideas and symbols, treating them as an extension of the self. He calls on us to "embark on the difficult journey" that's required to "gradually free oneself from the grip of unconscious culture."[6] He saw this as a transcendental challenge for humankind.

Hall was fascinated by how people use time and space, and he created categories of cultural comparison to describe these differences. Thus time could be experienced more *polychronically* (cyclical, situational) or more *monochronically* (linear, absolute). Hall studied cultural intuitions systematically and believed that bringing them into awareness was liberating. He felt that understanding culture frees us from blind adherence to social conventions.

Hall's work corresponded with a vast increase of intercultural contact, including the travel and exchange of World War II. Then in 1961, the U.S. government created the Peace Corps, which sent thousands of volunteers to live in foreign countries. The volunteers often underestimated the challenges of trying to adapt to life in vastly different cultural environments—so much so that many failed to complete their assignments. They lived through radical psychological shifts and profoundly transformational experiences such as culture shock, identity crises, and changes in values and life goals.

Hall understood that cultural learning had this transformational potential. Unfortunately, his ideas seem to excite relatively little interest today, even among intercultural specialists. Yet the challenges and opportunities that he described a half-century ago are now being faced by millions. Our globalized world provides a challenge of personal growth, and Hall gave us hints about how to go about it:

> *The reason man does not experience his true cultural self is that until he experiences another self as valid, he has little basis for validating his own self. A way to experience another group is to understand and accept the way their minds work. This is not easy. In fact, it is*

extraordinarily difficult, but it is of the essence of cultural understanding.[7]

Many researchers followed in Hall's footsteps in an attempt to understand cultural differences and the challenges of intercultural adaptation. They developed categories of comparison, such as *individualism* and *collectivism*, to help make sense of these mostly intuitive differences. For businesses, cultural misunderstanding can be expensive, so much of the research and training in intercultural communication has come from the world of business. Perhaps the most influential researcher in this area is the Dutch psychologist Geert Hofstede. Through research into cultural differences among IBM employees around the world, he created a schema for describing cultural difference that has become the standard for business schools around the world.[8]

The end of the twentieth century brought about other great advances in our understanding of culture, as researchers started to look at the intersection between culture and a variety of scientific disciplines. Cognitive scientists have gained a better understanding of the evolutionary underpinnings of brain function and a greater understanding of unconscious cognition,[9] social intelligence,[10] and even consciousness.[11] The study of genetics has allowed us to better trace human evolution, including the development of culture and language.[12] Research by social psychologists has taken the unconscious out of the realm of psychotherapy to focus on the out-of-awareness processes that underpin human behavior. In the next chapter, we'll catch up on current research about culture and the human brain. We'll see that, in important ways, Edward Hall was right—we are heavily influenced by cultural programming. And our sojourns can put us in touch with parts of ourselves of which we aren't normally aware.

CHAPTER SIX

Deep Culture
and
Cognition

TRADITIONALLY, INQUIRY INTO THE subjective side of life—mind, thought, feeling—was the domain of philosophers and poets. These days, researchers, particularly in the fields of psychology, neuroscience, and cognitive science, have made great inroads into understanding the biological underpinnings of the human experience. Their work is shedding light on the workings of the brain and giving us new avenues toward understanding the hidden processes of deep culture.

Our journey through some of the research in this area begins in ancient China with one of the most influential people in human history—K'ung-fu-tzu, known to Westerners as Confucius (see figure 6.1). Though he was a relatively unimportant government official and had few followers in his lifetime, his ideas have shaped the thinking of billions of people over two-and-a-half millennia.[1]

K'ung-fu-tzu (traditionally 551–479 BCE) lived at a time of political and social decline. As the minister of justice in the state of Lu, he wanted to encourage fairness, social stability, and personal morality. Coincidentally, it was around this

FIGURE 6.1   Confucius

time in Athens, Greece, that Plato founded his academy, which was dedicated to the pursuit of knowledge about the natural world and human affairs, including morality.

The thinking of Confucius and his contemporaries in China differed from that of the ancient Greeks. Confucius and Plato had, in effect, different approaches to thinking things through. Those differences have shaped values and collective thought processes up through the present day.[2] One of the most startling discoveries by modern-day cognitive scientists is that some of our most basic cognitive processes have been influenced by deep cultural difference that can be traced far into the past. We find evidence for this in research that compares the cognitive impact of contrasting worldviews. When cognitive scientists measure those differences, it's as though the voices of these ancient thinkers can be heard whispering in today's research laboratories.

CULTURE AND THOUGHT

Look at figure 6.2. If you were forced to choose, would you say that the cow belongs more naturally together with the chicken or with the grass?

Westerners (people from Western Europe and the United States) more often associate the cow with the chicken (based on them sharing a category—animals), while East Asians (Chinese and Japanese) relatively more often associate the cow with the grass (based on them sharing a relationship—cows eat grass). This is one of many experiments that have investigated how cultural differences in cognition form the underpinnings of differing cultural worldviews.

FIGURE 6.2   Category versus relationship

These results tie Americans and Europeans to the type of thinking that originated in ancient Greece. Plato believed that pure thought or "reasoning" could bring us toward absolute truths and help us identify essential qualities in the world around us. This emphasis on reason (as separate from emotion) encouraged the detachment of subject-object thinking. Plato's dialogues were written to show how reason was superior to the appeals to emotion used by the orators of the day, the Sophists. Even today, the word *sophistry* contains a whiff of condescension.

There were rationalists among the ancient Chinese, but they were never as influential as other thinkers, like Confucius, who assumed that it was futile to try to identify essential qualities using thought alone. Taijitsu, the symbol of the Yin and Yang of Taoism, perfectly illustrates the assumption that any quality contains within it the seeds of its opposite (see figure 6.3). Thus, the world is more than the sum total of its parts and can't be understood simply by separating things into elemental components. These insights were based on observations of patterns in nature—day turns to night, hot things get cold and cold things warm up, and so on. Chinese civilization, and East Asians in general, have been influenced this kind of context, relationship, and process-oriented thinking.

FIGURE 6.3   The Taijitsu

Contrasting cognitive styles aren't just apparent in the laboratory, but in the "real world" of legal systems, medical practice, contracts, social relations, and so on. Traditional Chinese medicine, for example, is predicated on seeing the body as a dynamic system that is sick when it is out of balance. Western medicine sees the body more as a sum total of all its parts (one identifies and treats the part that is sick). These views aren't mutually exclusive, yet they reflect differing thought traditions.

In Europe and the United States, there is a tendency to see social relations in terms of individuals who negotiate their place in society with other individuals. Individuals are the basic unit of social thought. In Asia (and much of the rest of the world, for that matter), society tends to be perceived in more organic terms, with individuals seen as forming part of a greater indivisible whole.

There are some who find these notions ludicrous. After all, how can one possibly say that all East Asians (billions of people!) and all Westerners (whatever that means!) think alike? This however is not the claim. The claim is only that deep culture affects some of our most fundamental thought processes.

When we grow up in a social world that values, for example, subject-object thinking, our minds can get comfortable with that approach to looking at things. This doesn't necessarily blind us to other alternatives. China has certainly adopted Western medical treatments, and many Westerners feel that Chinese medicine makes sense. These differences don't predetermine the way any individual will think—we can all see the cow as associated with the chicken or the grass. And you will find people in every culture who are more or less oriented toward particular thinking styles.

On the other hand, deep culture learners do report experiencing these differences firsthand. A German manager in Japan told me that it took him a year to understand the problem-solving approach of the Japanese engineers on his staff. At first he found them to be highly unsystematic and inefficient—they wanted to gather lots of data as a first step toward solving a problem. The German manager was used to breaking a problem down into parts at the beginning and using that as a starting point for gathering only necessary data. Later, he realized that the Japanese engineers expected the solution to emerge naturally from the data gathering process—which it often did. It was an equally effective yet less linear approach. He concluded that he became a better problem solver by increasing his cognitive flexibility.

DEEP CULTURE AND THE BRAIN

Deep culture is related to much more than information processing and problem solving. We are, in effect, animals that think. We have basic instincts and drives (we experience hunger), learn complex tasks to satisfy them (we cook food in elaborate ways), are driven by emotion (we get upset if our cooking isn't appreciated), and think abstractly and morally about what we do (we decide to buy organic produce). Our brain is a master integrator of these differing levels of experience.

This integration process is felt most obviously when the symbolic world of thought is connected to deeply felt emotions and drives. When Japanese warlords wanted to stamp out Christianity in the seventeenth century, Christian believers were forced to recant their faith and prove it by stepping on Christian symbols, such as the cross/crucifix. For many believers, performing this powerful symbolic act was impossible, and they lost their lives because of their unwillingness to do so. The symbol of their faith had to be respected even at the price of their own lives.

To understand the role of deep culture in how we experience the world, it helps to know a little about the structure of our brains. The different elements of our experience (thought, feelings, memory, imagination, and so on) are associated with particular areas of the brain. And different elements of our intercultural learning can be understood by taking a look at the brain's evolutionary architecture.

There are three interconnected yet distinct parts of the brain, each of which corresponds to stages of our biological evolution. It's as though we have three brains in one, each one adding newly developed functions onto previously developed ones. The *reptilian brain*, located at the base of the skull, is the oldest in evolutionary terms. It handles bodily functions such as breathing and heart rate and is relatively rigid in its functioning. The goal of this part of the brain is homeostasis, a stable internal state that allows for an organism's survival. Our deepest survival instincts are rooted here, and it's difficult to consciously regulate these automatic processes. This is why physical danger makes us "lose our heads" as we scramble to safety.

New experiences can stress our nervous system and the bodily functions controlled by our reptilian brain. You may feel vaguely threatened or overwhelmed standing in a crowded marketplace, surrounded by foreign sights and sounds. This may increase your heart rate, make your breathing shallower, cause you to sweat, cause loss of appetite, and so on. This happens because our higher cognitive processes are overwhelmed and put the body on high alert— ready to deal with any threat.

The midbrain, particularly the *limbic* system, can be thought of as the *mammalian brain*. It evolved later, is located on top of the reptilian brain, and is much more flexible in its functioning. It remembers experiences that were pleasurable, painful, or important. It produces emotion and is the seat of our value judgments. And while we feel the effects of the limbic system, it usually operates outside of our awareness. The emotional rush of falling in love, the anger we feel when insulted, the hesitation to touch something that burned us in the past—all these experiences originate in this part of the brain.

The limbic system is the platform on which deep culture is built. Our fundamental urges of territoriality and self-preservation are rooted there. It is also where our intellectual and symbolic world is connected to our more basic emotions and needs. The excitement of planning a wedding is related, at least in part, to an evolutionary imperative to find a mate and reproduce. When we use intellectual arguments to defend our ideas, we are defending psychological territory. At some fundamental level of brain functioning, we are not so unlike the family dog that is barking to keep strangers away from the yard.

This is an important point for deep culture learners. An intercultural experience is not simply an idea, it engages our animal nature as well. For example, we have deeply rooted physiological reactions to things that are perceived, even unconsciously, as disrespectful, threatening, or bizarre. The desecration of a sacred object can provoke true rage, and threats to our beliefs or values can provoke primal responses. Humans are the only species that is capable of feeling upset or excited about an idea—something that exists only as symbolic imagery in our minds.

On top of the limbic system is the *neocortex*, sometimes called the *primate brain*, which handles complex tasks. In humans, it has developed two large cerebral hemispheres that make us capable of abstract thought, language, and imagination. The neocortex is interconnected with other parts of the brain and participates in decoding sensory data, controlling voluntary movements, and creating a meaningful perceptual experience of the world. This "meaningful perceptual experience" is the world of the mind. The mind helps us navigate our physical and social realities, all the while relying heavily on the mental maps of deep culture.

THE DEEP CULTURE AUTOPILOT

Our new understanding of the brain helps us to understand our everyday experience of reality, including previously mysterious areas like consciousness and the unconscious mind. Sigmund Freud saw the unconscious mind primarily as a source of primitive emotions and motivations. But today's cognitive scientists are beginning to understand that there is another vast realm of unconscious activity in our minds. This newly appreciated aspect of brain function is critical to our understanding of deep culture.

Specialists use the term *cognitive unconscious* to describe our brain's "autopilot."[4] This autopilot manages our automatic interactions with our environment. When you drive, for example, your cognitive unconscious takes care of the routine tasks. You accelerate, change lanes, and make your way down the road automatically. If you take the same route home every day, your autopilot may even choose your freeway exit for you. The split between your conscious mind and cognitive unconscious manifests itself in your ability to plan dinner while driving home. While we can only pay conscious attention to one thing at a time, we can simultaneously pay unconscious attention to another.

The cognitive unconscious has multiple functions: information filter, pattern recognizer, implicit learner, and feeling evaluator. It is active in motivation as well. Yet despite its importance, we seldom notice how much we rely on it to get through the day. It ties your shoes in the morning, sends you to the refrigerator for breakfast, greets your colleagues automatically, tells you when someone is being rude, adjusts language use to the appropriate level of politeness, and so on, and so on, and so on.

But the cognitive unconscious doesn't control our lives. We aren't, after all, simply following unconscious urges. We also have a *narrative conscious* mind produced by the cerebral hemispheres of the neocortex. This is the part of our mind that "pays attention." We experience it as a string of thoughts and intentional consideration of problems or situations. This includes the sense that we are observers of our own internal processes.

The narrative conscious and cognitive unconscious work seamlessly in tandem. The cognitive unconscious is continually scanning the environment, recognizing patterns, responding automatically, and sending information to the narrative conscious to be dealt with. For example, if someone suddenly cuts you off in traffic, your cognitive unconscious reflexively swerves the car out of the way as your narrative conscious forms the thought, "What a jerk!" Your conscious mind can then take over your actions and think through what you should do about the situation. Perhaps it tells you to suppress your anger and forget about it. The process is illustrated in figure 6.5.

The cognitive unconscious is closely tied to our emotions and instincts—not in the way that Freud described, but in the fundamental urges and sensations that are key to our survival. The car swerving in front of us provokes the same adrenaline rush and fear that the appearance of a dangerous animal did 100,000 years ago. In fact, these responses are so fundamental to our biology that they take place independently of activity in the part of the brain responsible for reasoning and abstract thought. This means that your cognitive unconscious started to swerve your car

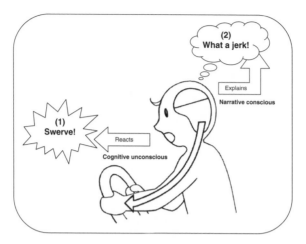

FIGURE 6.4   The narrative conscious and cognitive unconscious

even before your conscious mind had access to the knowledge of what was happening. That's why it's so hard to stifle our "gut responses" provoked by new people and places we don't understand.

I have talked about the cognitive unconscious in terms of emotion and instinctive reactions to our environment. But our autopilot does much more than handle routine actions and instinctive emotional responses. We must navigate both the physical world of objects and the social universe of human community. That universe is symbolic and abstract. For example, the things we take pride in and defend—whether horsepower, a promotion, justice, or love—are simply ideas. But these ideas are part of the social reality experienced in the collective mind of our community.

To manage your interaction with that social reality, your cognitive unconscious autopilot needs a rich template of information—one that takes years to learn as we grow up. These "communal maps" are what help us make sense of the wedding that we discussed in chapter 2. Although the mental universe within our cognitive unconscious is a symbolic representation of the world, for all practical purposes it *is* the world we live in. We are attached emotionally to it and react to a threat to our worldview with a fight-or-flight response. People are ready to fight for a bigger paycheck or even die for ideals. The symbolic world *is* our "real" world, and our survival instinct is intent on protecting and perpetuating it.

THE UNCONSCIOUS MIND AND DEEP CULTURE LEARNING

So what does all this brain work mean for deep culture learners?

Our cognitive unconscious is fast—but stupid. It's good at swerving your car, but needs help from the conscious mind to make sense of immediate problems. You may find that even walking through unfamiliar streets can be cognitively exhausting. The narrative conscious is darting here and there trying to make sense of things, while the cognitive unconscious tries to recognize and absorb implicit patterns.

We experience this process as a series of observations and thoughts that we have about them. Our autopilot picks out unfamiliar patterns in our environment. For example, riding the subway when I first lived in Japan, I found the silence of the packed trains unnerving and unnatural. My narrative conscious pondered what this meant about Japanese people. The danger here, of course, is jumping to easy yet inaccurate conclusions in an attempt to render out new environment predictable.

In terms of our lived experience, our brain is a meaning-making organ. In a new environment, this meaning-making process is more difficult. Stereotypes and generalizations are one shortcut that our brain uses to make sense of things. But if we make ethnocentric judgments, our brain can be primed to find patterns that confirm our prejudices. These confirmations harden our attitudes so that cultural learning becomes difficult or impossible. This can lead to *cynical expat syndrome*, in which long-term residents spout highly prejudiced judgments about their host community. Yet from the point of view of these expatriates, they are simply reporting the facts—truths that they have "confirmed" through long experience.

One long-term American resident of Japan I know has maintained for years that Japanese people will never accept foreigners as equals. He calls Japanese society exclusionary and marshals personal experiences to justify his conclusions. For example, he argues that some landlords hesitate to rent to foreigners, and that there are no equal housing laws to mandate otherwise. Yet this individual speaks very little Japanese and makes almost no attempt to develop deeper relationships with Japanese people. He lives in an expatriate cocoon. His conclusion that Japanese exclude foreigners precludes him from deep culture learning. And he maintains these attitudes in spite of knowing people, like me, who are very well integrated into Japanese society and don't feel it to be excessively exclusionary.

We are especially likely to draw prejudicial conclusions when we have a negative emotional response to an experience. Someone from Finland (which has a very reserved communication style) who visits Egypt (where communication is more expressive) may instinctively find people "pushy" or "aggressive." These are not just thoughts; they are whole-body reactions. To avoid letting these initial responses turn into prejudices, we need to be aware of our mental and emotional processes. We have little control over our gut responses to a situation, but we can suspend judgment and give our minds the time to create a more nuanced interpretation.

An understanding of our mental processes also explains why it can be so hard to learn to speak foreign languages well or fully integrate into other societies. Once our deep culture mind maps have been imprinted, they stay there. You never (or almost never) forget your native language and never lose your deep culture settings. To function in a new environment, you must, to some degree, start over again. This means constructing a new worldview that corresponds to that of your host community. It can be a painstaking step-by-step process.

The genius of the brain's design is that it is remarkably plastic when we are growing up and remarkably stable afterward. But this also results in *ethnocentrism*. We naturally categorize people in terms of "us" versus "them." Loyalty to our community and its ideals is important for human survival, since that is what allows us to collaborate and ultimately survive. Ethnocentrism shouldn't surprise us, but it often gets in the way of cultural learning. And when our natural tendency toward ethnocentrism is combined with societal attitudes of prejudice, the results can be discrimination, war, or even genocide.

We face significant cognitive challenges as deep culture learners. We need a sort of detached engagement: the ability to try new things without passing judgment too quickly. As we'll see in the next chapter, not everyone is able to do this. Those who do, however, find that our sojourns transform not only our interpretation of the people in other places, but our view of the world itself.

CHAPTER SEVEN

Deep Culture
and
Intercultural Sensitivity

LET'S TAKE OUR UNDERSTANDING of deep culture on the road!

We've been talking about deep culture mostly as an abstraction. But our real goal is to get more out of experiences abroad—to explore our inner terrain as we explore the world. With this in mind, I'd like to introduce two people who have been affected by intercultural experiences. Ludovic is a Frenchman who spent five years hitchhiking around the world. He arrived back in France after traveling through fifty-seven countries and covering 170,000 kilometers (105,000 miles)—through rain, snow, desert, dust, and storm. He used only free transportation and interacted continually with locals. He created a blog to share the adventures and the life lessons that he learned.[1] Ludovic returned home talking not about cultural difference and diversity, but about the commonalities that he discovered among people everywhere.

Yuko is another world traveler who has had remarkable intercultural experiences.[2] She was raised in India by Japanese parents, attended international schools, and learned to speak Hindi, Japanese, and English. She went on to study in the United States and Europe, and moved back to Japan in her early twenties. Yuko is a chameleon, shifting effortlessly between languages and communication styles. Though she was raised and educated abroad and experienced little of Japan, she has reintegrated herself so well to life there that her Japanese friends are sometimes surprised to learn that she speaks English—much less that she wasn't raised in Japan. Yet Yuko hasn't given up her international self; she shifts back and forth between multiple cultural worlds and reports that she is ultimately most at home in this between-state.

Of the two, who is more international? Put more precisely, what are the cultural lessons learned by Ludovic and Yuko? This question is important, because Ludovic's and Yuko's experiences may show us our own possibilities for cultural learning. What deeper lessons did they learn, beyond the knowledge of how to get along in particular places? Did Ludovic learn more because he spent time in more places? Does he thus have a better understanding of cultural diversity? Did he develop more tolerance because of the extreme situations he encountered? But perhaps Yuko gained a flexibility in thinking and communicating that Ludovic didn't. He didn't have the time, after all, to learn foreign languages and deeply understand the places he visited.

Curiously, there's little consensus even among experts on how to define a successful intercultural experience. Some different measures that have been suggested are the ability to function in another society, one's satisfaction with one's stay, the formation of relationships, knowledge of one's host community, or hard to define goals such as "cultural awareness." It's hard to say which of these are of fundamental or core importance. Determining what our learning goals might be when we set off on a sojourn can be more difficult than it first appears.

The person who helped me cut through this confusion is Milton Bennett. He has created a definition of successful learning that I find extremely useful and that goes well with what we've been learning about deep culture's influence in our lives. He uses the term *intercultural sensitivity*, which he defines as "the construction of reality as increasingly capable of accommodating cultural difference."[3] According to Bennett, intercultural experiences bring us into contact with cultural difference, which must be interpreted and dealt with in some way. If we can accept that these differences represent a valid yet alternative way of looking at things, we are able to accommodate them into our view of reality. Bennett describes six stages that we go through as we learn to do this.[4] Eventually we may learn to construct alternative worldviews—that is, gain the ability to look at the world from multiple cultural perspectives.

This definition is rather abstract. Perhaps it's easier to think of intercultural sensitivity as a sort of cognitive flexibility toward cultural difference. Rather than inflexibly sticking to our normal way of perceiving things, we enter into the perceptual world of others. Intercultural sensitivity does not automatically make us function well in a new environment, become satisfied with our experiences, or give us knowledge of our host community—but it does make those things easier. Bennett's ideas match my experiences very well. Living in Mexico, I felt a cognitive shift as I improved my Spanish, made friends, did business, and interacted with people. I started to have a greater awareness of cultural difference and developed a sense of the worldview of my new home.

These ideas can give us a new way to look at Yuko's and Ludovic's experiences. We can ask ourselves, "How did their perceptions of cultural difference shift as a result of their experiences?" and "To what degree were they able to enter into the perceptual world of their hosts?" Given the way that they describe their experiences, we can guess that Ludovic hasn't been able to look at the worldviews of the places he visited from the inside. He simply didn't have enough time in any given place. And Ludovic talks about his cultural lessons in terms of shared humanity rather than shifting perception. Yuko, on the other hand, seems to see perceive other cultural worlds more fully—even shifting among different cultural selves.

I believe that intercultural sensitivity is an important goal of deep culture learning. But as Ludovic's experience hints, it isn't something that is gained quickly or easily, even if we spend as much time traveling as he did. We need longer, more involved experiences in order to fully explore the way of thinking in another cultural community. The mental habits of deep culture are not so easily reprogrammed.

Even with a longer stay, the process of gaining intercultural sensitivity is not automatic. I have talked to hundreds of people about their reactions to cultural difference. After a short time in a new country, people will often tell me that they "basically" understand their host community. In a sense, perhaps this is true. They've been there, learned how things look, and seen the people that live there. But often they haven't made much progress toward gaining a new cultural perspective. They are simply reporting on the impressions of their host community based on the standards they've brought from home.

But let's not be too harsh. Ethnocentrism is not a moral failing. It's part of our evolutionary heritage and it's not easy to recognize or overcome. Just as we can never overcome egocentrism (we will never be fully selfless in our daily dealings with others), neither will we ever achieve an absolutely transcendent intercultural state. The goal is not a superior way of looking at cultural difference, but rather the willingness to keep expanding our perspective.

EMPATHY AND JUDGMENT

To consciously move toward a state of increased intercultural sensitivity, I recommend that sojourners cultivate *deep culture empathy*. That is, in our travels we should attempt to look at the world through the eyes of our hosts. This may sound simple. We would all like to think that we understand how other people look at the world, but deep culture empathy requires more than adopting an intellectual stance of tolerance for diversity. As in any relationship, to truly accept someone you must first learn about him or her. You need to step outside of your world and into another.

Almost everyone has experienced at least some degree of cultural empathy. When you return from a vacation, even a short one, you probably see your home town, maybe even your neighborhood and house, in a new way. For a time anyway, you look at your normal world as a bit of an outsider. When you show visitors around your city and explain local sites, you may find that you are focusing on how *they* see your home and what they might find interesting. This perceptual shift is cultural empathy.

People with a high degree of cultural empathy are able to consciously shift cultural perspectives—a kind of cultural *code switching* (a linguistics term that refers to switching between languages during a single conversation). Some interculturalists experience a shift not only in language, but in worldview. A Senegalese friend who lives in France, for example, described to me the feeling of "putting on my Senegalese glasses when in Senegal and my French glasses when I'm in France." This conscious shift into a different way of viewing the world requires one to understand the insider's perspective of multiple cultural realities. But it doesn't come easily or quickly. In Ludovic's case for example, he has traveled widely and may be extremely tolerant of extreme environments, yet he hasn't had the opportunity to stay in one place long enough to start gaining the deeper perspective of a cultural insider.

Yuko, on the other hand, has had very deep experiences in the places she has lived. She has had to reconcile within herself: (1) a Hindi-speaking self comfortable in India, (2) an outspoken English-speaking internationalist, and (3) a Japanese self who gets along in a traditional Japanese environment. What Ludovic learned was wide in scope but shallow in substance, while Yuko learned lessons that are more narrow but deep. Ludovic saw a lot, but never had the time to look beyond the surface of new streets, food, buildings, gestures, and clothes. Yuko reports that it took her three years back in Japan to learn to eat noodles slurping in the proper Japanese style. She went through fundamental transformations as she learned to communicate, make friends, work, and be at home in different places.

While Ludovic certainly learned a lot, I think Yuko's experiences serve as a better example of the possibilities of deep culture learning. How does it feel to live in this state? Yuko reports that although she shifts between different worlds, her multiple selves are integrated into an organic whole. She expresses her personality and makes moral choices in the context of understanding different ways of perceiving a situation. She gets along with many different types of people and uses her wide range of social and cultural skills to her advantage. She can lower her head or speak up as she chooses.

Developing deep cultural empathy involves personal transformation at many levels. Emotionally, it helps us become flexible, accepting, and curious. Cognitively, it helps us learn to look at things from a variety of perspectives; to "read" the expectations of a new environment, the logic of others' thinking, and the interests of all involved in a given situation. There are few absolutes, which can be a powerful tool for understanding. Yet this can also lead to unsettling questions.

CULTURAL IDENTITY AND VALUES—WHO AM I?

Deep culture learning can set us adrift. In my case, I started living abroad and felt little desire to return to my home country. Yet I didn't feel that I had truly found a new home. Changing countries and learning another language excited me for several years, but I had a nagging feeling that my life was fractured—broken into pieces that couldn't be made whole. In Mexico I was a *gringo*, though well integrated into the community. In Japan I was a *gaijin*, though one who spoke Japanese and functioned well in society. In France I didn't stand out physically, so I felt frustrated that my non-native French marked me as a foreigner. Visiting my original home in the United States, I felt a bit like a spy—someone who has a hidden life and ulterior motives.

Many people experience similar feelings of disconnect as a result of deep culture learning. Students who study abroad for a year often tell me that they return home a different person, but their family and old friends don't notice.

At a welcome-home party, people ask politely how life was abroad, but have trouble staying interested in the answer for more than a few minutes. Upon return, sojourners are expected to slide right back in to their old selves, but they can't, because their perspective of the world has undergone a fundamental shift.

Deep culture empathy also raises questions about what's important to us. Sometimes we idealize the lifestyle or values of our new home. I found the extended networks and loyalties of Mexican families to be wonderfully nurturing and started feeling that "family" as I knew it in the United States was dysfunctional. In Japan, I found people's ability to cooperate a refreshing change from the let-me-tell-you-why-I'm-special individualism I was used to. In time, I got over these negative attitudes of my own country. And I hope I don't idealize my host communities. Yet this still left me with uncertainty about where I belonged and what was important to me as an individual.

Issues of belonging and values revolve around our sense of *identity*. In the simplest terms, this refers to how we answer the question, "Who am I?" As individuals we answer this question based on our tastes, profession, values, hobbies, and so on. As cultural learners, the question of who we are becomes more complicated. On a sojourn, we discover that we need to also develop a *cultural identity*. I was surprised in Mexico how people saw me first as an American and second as an individual. From their point of view, I was the United States of America. Even as I started to feel connected to Mexico, I was perceived as belonging to a place that was part of me, but also far away.

Our sense of personal and cultural identity revolves around our intuitive sense of the inside and outside of life spaces. All living things have boundaries: amoebas mediate what is inside their boundaries, and many animals have territory that they control and defend. Humans also experience selfness in terms of psychological territory. Teenagers sometimes struggle to define their own personal identities in relation to their families and larger society. For sojourners, the questions of cultural identity raised by deep culture learning mean that we need to define, demark, or defend our own sense of personal and cultural territory. We must develop a sense of where we belong, the values we want to live by, the kind of person we want to be, how we want to communicate, and so on.

This can put deep cultural learners into a bind. They may come to know different worlds that exist very separately. Children of immigrants or multicultural marriages often deal with conflicting expectations and values between family and the local community. Ethnic minorities may need to learn to code switch between different communication styles and values as they go back and forth between their community and the larger society. And those who live abroad must somehow resolve the sense of belonging to a new community with the disconnect they feel with their original home. Often the people back home just don't understand what life is like for them.

Grappling with these issues can lead to feelings of *marginality* — the sense that one doesn't belong anywhere.[5] Fortunately, there are ways to feel connected even without fully belonging to a single cultural world. Yuko talks about it in terms of being a chameleon; deep cultural learners have the ability to change appearances (behavior), yet maintain an underlying self that remains constant. Others have talked about the feeling of being a bridge between islands (see figure 7.1), solidly connected to more than one place, with a sense of self evolving from participation in life on multiple islands. In addition, the bridge has a unique vantage point from which to view the islands.

FIGURE 7.1   Bridging different cultures

I am sometimes asked for advice by those who have trouble integrating different cultural selves. I tell them that we connect by caring about the people and places we know. I recommend that people keep up long-distance networks and actively maintain relationships with people who link us to places that are important to us. After all, a multicultural identity is constructed, not discovered. I also recommend that people find appropriate ways to share their struggle with local friends in an effort to connect them in some way to the more distant parts of themselves. This could be as simple as talking about one's family members back home, or as complex as opening dialogues with local friends about feelings of not completely fitting in. Ultimately, cultural identity issues are resolved through connections that we consciously create and cultivate.

I sometimes feel that my life is like a multiplex—a theater in which several movies run at the same time. Each of the cultural worlds that I participate in is simply one movie out of the many that exist—more so than I will ever fully realize. And while many people live all their lives within a single room showing one movie, I move back and forth between different theaters, sharing the story in each with the people there. When asked where I feel that I most belong, I say that it's not in any of the particular theaters—it's in the multiplex itself. And walking the halls from one movie to another, knowing that each numbered door has a whole world behind it, is a privilege and a thrill.

WHY DEEP CULTURE LEARNING IS HARD

I've spoken of identity questions almost as though they are an unavoidable result of intercultural experience. But that would be an overstatement. Many people live abroad for years without questioning who they are. Indeed, living abroad can reinforce one's sense of cultural superiority. I know expatriates who are permanent residents in Japan, married to Japanese spouses, who insist on sending their children to international schools because they fear them becoming "too Japanese." I see privileged expatriates in less economically developed countries who view their posting as a hardship or little more than a necessary step on the career ladder. When sojourners are not forced to adapt to their local host community, deep culture learning can slow down significantly.

One intriguing study done in Australia showed how subtle and stubborn deep culture learning challenges can be. The study attempted to find out whether Australian students learned deep culture lessons during time spent living in France.[5] More specifically, researchers looked at how students dealt with deep culture differences in information-gathering strategies.

At Australian universities, gathering information is quite systematic—you find out regulations and requirements from the course catalogue, you find course offerings and schedules on the website, and so on. It's very transparent, but it tends to be impersonal and sometimes quite rigid, especially if you miss a deadline or need an exception to the rules. At French universities, information gathering is often a more personalized process. The official policies are only the starting point. Administrators often have more authority to waive rules and make special exceptions. On the other hand, the system is less transparent, so you need to ask around, find the right person to speak to, and perhaps spend time cultivating good relationships with those "in the know." These contrasting strategies are sometimes referred to as *universalistic* (low context, focused on systems and predictability) or *particularistic* (high context, focused on case-by-case flexibility).

This is a good example of deep culture difference hidden in plain sight. Australian students dealt regularly with the French university and had opportunities to uncover, bit by bit, hidden cultural patterns. Once they returned to Australia, they were asked to offer advice to future participants of the study-abroad program. Ideally, they would grasp not only that finding information in the French university involved different strategies than in Australia, but they would connect this difference to the larger context of French cultural tendencies.

So how did they do?

By some measures, very well. Overwhelmingly, students described their experiences in France in positive terms. On the other hand, when asked what they learned about information gathering at the French university, results were clearly negative. Many expressed deep frustration and were highly critical about the French administration, finding it disorderly and inefficient. Even the students who discovered effective strategies (getting to know administrators, for example) couched their lessons in terms of dealing with the "inefficiency" of the French system.

The conclusions that the Australian students drew about the French in this area were highly critical (and ethnocentric). In general, they weren't able to go beyond their personal frustration at being unable to do things in the way they were used to. Their response was to blame their new environment without noticing that their frustrations were based on hidden cultural conventions. Students frequently spouted negative judgments and generalizations like, "Always remember that the French are totally disorganized."

It should be pointed out that French students at Australian universities can also find information gathering highly inefficient. It can be difficult, for example, to find someone to answer your questions or give you personalized advice. You may simply be told, "Look it up in the course catalog." French students also need to learn a different way of "working the system" to get the information that they need.

The experience of these students illustrates perhaps the most difficult challenge of deep culture learning—simply recognizing hidden cultural patterns for what they are. To do so requires an ongoing, nonjudgmental engagement. We must be perceptive observers of our environment, cultivate the ability to withhold judgment, and examine our own discomfort in a detached manner.

PATIENCE, TRIAL, AND ERROR

There are other challenges to deep culture learning: one is that it takes time. It would have been impossible for the Australian students to discover the hidden patterns of deep culture in France by making a single attempt at getting information. Hidden patterns emerge only by using a trial-and-error approach to getting things done and understanding one's situation. And even then, we may miss patterns unless we are specifically paying attention.

Deep culture learning requires having the patience to take this trial-and-error approach. As soon as we make negative judgments about the differences we find to be unreasonable (in this case "inefficient"), we may give up trying or find that our negative experiences reinforce our prejudice. The ability to accept, to recognize difference without making negative value judgments, is important. Whether we like or dislike what we find, the first goal is to simply try and understand things *as they are.*

Successful deep culture learning requires more than simply judging one's own experience to be a success. The Australian students *did* learn a lot and felt their experiences to be valuable. And, of course, they are right. But they often failed to gain an insider's view of the situation. To that extent, their deep culture learning was stunted. Many of them had negative judgments reinforced, and they failed to learn about their own cultural programming.

GENERALIZATIONS, STEREOTYPES, AND PREJUDICE

To survive in a new environment, sojourners must make sense of new, sometimes seemingly inexplicable behaviors or attitudes. This can result in overgeneralizations. When I lived in Mexico, I initially drew the conclusion that "in Mexico people don't care if you are late." But I made the mistake of overgeneralizing based on a few experiences and a limited intuitive grasp of how time was being used. Eventually, I started to better understand the logic of *situational time* (see chapter 9 for more about this). I noticed, for example, that laborers who worked for an archeologist friend of mine arrived well before the appointed time to avoid keeping the boss waiting. I learned that if you ran into someone you knew by chance, the importance of your relationship with that person could be demonstrated by how much time he or she gave you. The way that time was prioritized followed expectations that were much more subtle and complex than my rather limited first set of conclusions.

Generalizations are sometimes confused with stereo-types, which are in turn sometimes confused with prejudice. A *generalization* is a statement of an overall tendency, which may or may not apply to a particular case. The statement "Japanese take off their shoes when they enter the house" is a generalization. It attempts to describe what is normal or typical, not what happens every time a Japanese enters the house. When we have just arrived in a new place, our brain may draw overly broad conclusions based on limited experiences. As long as we keep an open mind, we can modify our understanding as we go.

A *stereotype* is a way of categorizing someone by using a simple label or assigning an absolute trait. It is a way of describing what *is*—some essential quality that is assumed to belong to all members of a particular group. Stereotypes may have an element of truth: "Eskimos live in igloos." Stereotypes can be positive ("Americans are friendly") or negative ("Americans are shallow"). They can reflect racism and prejudice: "Blacks are lazy" or "Jews are stingy." But they can also be used playfully and even as a first step in communicating between different groups. In Hawaii, a very tolerant, multicultural environment, stereotypes about *Haoles* (whites), Hawaiians, Pacific Islanders, and Japanese are tossed around among locals as a form of banter. Importantly, though, they are seldom used to insult or demean a particular people.

The brain's ability to make split-second assignations based on in-group or out-group, social category, status, gender, and other characteristics is a fundamental part of our perceptual and evolutionary hardware. In that sense, we will never get rid of generalizations and stereotypes. One danger, however, is that when we use them to denigrate, we can fall into prejudice, holding negative a priori beliefs or judgments about groups or categories of people. *Prejudice* is a negative assumption or attitude that we bring with us into a given situation, independent of the particular circumstances. Put into practice, prejudice creates discrimination and unfair treatment. It probably has its psychological roots in an unconscious need to defend against a perceived threat.

For sojourners, generalizations are a necessary part of the trial-and-error process of cultural learning. Stereotypes are by definition inaccurate, but are hard to avoid since our mind naturally wants to categorize the people we interact with. Even prejudice is difficult to avoid entirely, since we often learn it unconsciously and may not recognize it. For example, research into *implicit associations* shows that many people have negative reactions to people of particular races.[7]

The biggest check on the negative consequences of overgeneralizations, stereotypes, and prejudice is an ability to suspend judgment. This keeps us from jumping to conclusions too quickly and helps us make more accurate observations about our new environment. We need to be aware of our own internal processes, as well, and notice the conclusions that our mind is drawing from our experiences. Culture learning involves reordering our way of looking at things at a deep level, so it shouldn't be surprising that it takes time and isn't always easy.

CULTURE SURPRISE, STRESS, AND SHOCK

Restructuring our view of the world can be an energy-consuming and stressful process. The term *culture shock* is widely known and often used to refer to our reaction to the unexpected and disconcerting things we find when abroad. But the term was originally meant to describe the psychological stresses of adapting to very different cultural environments, typical of extreme sojourns such as those made by volunteers in the Peace Corps. People have a whole range of reactions to new environments, and it's difficult to generalize, but there has been plenty of research that can help us better manage the challenges of our own deep culture learning.[8]

There are three different categories of adaptive stress. *Culture surprise* refers to the feeling of novelty that we initially experience in a new place. We realize that people are speaking a different language, their clothes are different, cars are driven on the other side of the street, the food is exotic, the marketplaces seem chaotic. Culture surprise is the "Wow!" effect of our initial impressions, and it normally wears off pretty quickly. In a matter of days we may feel at home, at least to some degree, in our host environment. But culture surprise can be stressful when we find the food hard to eat, the language impossible to understand, the streets confusing, and the people indecipherable. We then may seek the comforts of familiar food, the resort hotel pool, or long e-mails to friends back home.

Beyond our initial culture surprise comes *culture stress*. This refers not so much to the shock of novelty, but to the stress of trying to function in our new community. The simplest of activities, such as buying a train ticket or shopping for food, can be terribly time- and energy-consuming.

Nothing works as we expect. Our cognitive unconscious becomes overloaded with sensory input and unrecognizable patterns, and our conscious problem-solving mind is taxed to exhaustion. We may be in the country we've been dreaming of, only to find that we have no desire to leave our room. As their stay continues, most people soon learn to meet the needs of daily life. But in fact, this level of adaption is mostly on the surface; it involves using relatively easy-to-learn procedures for getting what we want. We learn how to shop, use public transportation, and so on. But with a longer stay, we may find that a deeper, harder to define adaptive stress remains.

Culture shock, as I use it, refers to the deeper malaise that comes from a longer-term stay. The longer we are in a new place, and the more we learn about it, the more we face adaptive choices and the limits of our flexibility. How much can I or should I change myself to get along in this place? How do I feel about the people, the values, and the lifestyles here? Why am I here? This accumulation of cultural stress can lead to a state of mental or emotional detachment, irritation—even sickness, depression, or anxiety.

The literature on culture shock generally portrays it as a natural process that people recover from as a matter of course. And I agree in the sense that most people eventually recover a sense of normalcy. Yet culture shock is also a sign that we have, temporarily at least, reached our adaptive limits. In my experience, some people react to this by retreating into an isolated existence or expatriate community from which they never emerge. They are, in effect, biding their time until they can return to normal life back home. Or, they create a cocoon that attempts to integrate the parts of the host community that they like and avoid the things they don't.

What a shame! Cultural adaptability is like a muscle: the more you use it the stronger it gets. The mark of a deep culture learner is not that he or she doesn't experience culture shock (I certainly always have) but the ability to not blame the host culture for his or her own difficulties. A deep culture learner is self-aware and recognizes that negative reactions are part of a learning process that enriches us. Despite the challenges, we keep coming back for more. And it is this insistence on accepting a cultural world on its own terms that has the power to transform our experience of the world.

The challenges of the Australian students in France capture an important lesson for us. To get the most out of our experiences we must not only seek an understanding of our new environment, but try to understand the deep culture learning process itself. We need to place our own reactions to our environment into the larger context of change and learning that we are going through. In the next chapter, we'll take a closer look at the deep culture learning process so that we'll be able to recognize it in ourselves and others.

CHAPTER EIGHT

Resistance, Acceptance, *and* Adaptation

I LOVE HEARING THE STORIES that sojourners tell about their experiences abroad. I'm often struck by the variety of reactions people have to the challenges of dealing with cultural difference. Some seem to learn a lot and feel very positive about their experiences; others seem detached, critical of their hosts, or even stubbornly oblivious. I meet people who've lived abroad for years in isolated expatriate cocoons, and others who delve deeply into the language and society of their new home. But what's the difference? Why do some people adapt and learn, while others do not? Why do some people get so much more out of their experiences than others do?

One obvious answer is that people's situations vary widely. And some people are more open and curious than others. Perhaps the diversity of experience and personality make this question unanswerable. But if we can't know the *why* of these diverse reactions, we can at least look more closely at the *how*—at the different ways that people react to the challenges of deep culture learning. So let's take a brief look at the cultural learning process as I understand it, with an eye toward understanding how it plays out for each individual. My hope is that this will help us better manage our own deep culture learning.

SURFACE AND DEEP EXPERIENCES

The starting point for understanding the process of cultural adaptation and learning is the recognition that cultural experiences can be relatively more *surface* or *deep*. A surface experience is one that involves dealing with obvious cultural difference such as new food, transportation systems, and so on. The adaptive challenges of a surface experience usually involve following some established procedure, such as "Take off your shoes when entering the temple" or "Hold your chopsticks this way."

A deep experience involves engagement with more hidden, abstract layers of cultural difference. Deep experiences require ongoing trial-and-error learning. We start to understand values, communication styles, and how to read a situation or behavior. To speak a foreign language well requires a deep culture understanding of the cultural world of its speakers. At the beginning of my stay in France, I learned phrases for ordering in a restaurant (a surface experience), and as my stay progressed I started to better understand the subtleties of talking to and forming good relationships with French waiters (a deeper experience). My relationship with my French partner and her family uncovered even deeper cultural patterns, such as expectations about the roles between parents and children.

Dealing with surface cultural difference can be a challenge (shopping in a foreign language, searching in vain for the right bus), but in general, surface experiences affect us less than deeper ones. Deeper cultural experiences, on the other hand, are harder to articulate, but often more meaningful. You can learn about this difference by asking someone who has been traveling or living abroad, "What kind of cultural difference did you notice?" or "What did you learn while you were there?" By listening to how people talk about their experiences, and in particular their reactions to cultural difference, you can learn to judge the depth of their experiences.

First, notice whether they refer to visible elements of the environment they were in—the architecture, food, or weather. If so, they are reporting a surface experience.[1] The lessons learned from surface experiences are often concrete and easily expressed, such as, "Well, we found that the southern coast was magnificent," "The Picasso museum was marvelous," or "I learned to eat with chopsticks!" At times however, even surface experiences resonate deeply and make even short trips abroad highly meaningful. You may hear, "Oh, seeing beggars was shocking."

By *surface experience* I don't mean shallow and inconsequential experience. "Surface" refers to the more visible side of culture. If we spend only a few weeks away, or spend our time in sheltered expatriate communities, we deal with only the most explicit elements of a place: the food, transportation systems, architecture, greetings, and so on. Our interaction with people is more limited and often not in the local language. We are the outsider looking at the surface of things. As I've heard Milton Bennett say, "An American tourist in Japan isn't having a Japanese experience. He's having an *American experience in Japan!*"[2]

If you ask people who have lived for longer periods abroad these questions, they will more often talk about the life they had in the host community—the friends they made, the new perspective they have gained, and the challenge of integrating, learning the host language, or dealing with parts of the experience they found difficult. For some, the experience will have been transformational—the person he or she is today is different than the one he or she was before their journey. These are *deeper experiences* that are a reflection of a fuller engagement with cultural difference. These sojourners have engaged with the trial-and-error process of learning to participate in the cultural world of their hosts.

Surface experiences can be extremely meaningful and may affect our lives in important ways. We may have wonderful interactions and feel deeply moved by how we're received. We may see sacred places and be greatly inspired. But these experiences are different from deep culture learning. Short-term travel inspires us by reinforcing things that, at some level, we knew already. Deep culture learning, on the other hand, involves grappling with the unknown, allowing oneself to adapt, and slowly constructing an expanded sense of the world.

Deep culture learning often involves extensive adaptation to our new environment, including learning a new language, making new friends, communicating in new ways, and coming to understand new values. It may also involve inner conflict as we try to integrate different ways of looking at things. And while deep culture learning is profound, we often don't notice consciously that it's happening. It happens in the background as we learn the subtleties of the host language, form deeper friendships, and adapt to a new working style, sense of time, way of solving problems, and so on. Our attention isn't focused on personal insights; it's focused on gaining entry into the world as it's experienced by the people who live in this new place.

ADAPTIVE DEMANDS

At the root of both surface and deep culture experiences is the fundamental need for us to deal with the *adaptive demands* imposed on us by our new environment. By definition, we don't function as well in our new environment as we do back home. We have to learn new things: how to use the subway, order food, conjugate verbs, disagree without being rude, and so on. Our normal habits and patterns are insufficient. We must change.

But change is stressful and requires that we adjust our psychological boundaries. We are like an amoeba that finds its internal state is out of kilter with its outer environment. When possible, amoebas change their internal structure to match their outside world, or else try to prevent destructive foreign elements from entering them. Cultural learning is similar in that we must find a way to deal with the gap between what we know already (our internal state) and the demands of our new home (our external environment).

As I see it, there are three possible reactions to adaptive demands. We can actively *resist* changing ourselves to match our environment; we can *accept* and recognize the demands as valid yet choose not to change; or we can *adapt*, and change something within ourselves (gain new knowledge, skills, behaviors, and points of view) in order to bring our internal state into closer balance with the demands of our environment.

In chapter 7, I said that we develop intercultural sensitivity by integrating cultural difference into our view of the

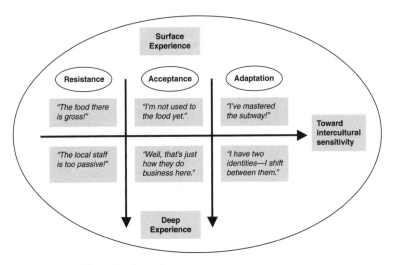

FIGURE 8.1   The cultural learning process

world. Resisting, accepting, and adapting to demands are at the core of this process. When we resist the cultural difference we find, we are effectively refusing to integrate them into our view of what's normal. By accepting the differences we find, we allow ourselves to become less ethnocentric and to more easily internalize new cultural patterns. Adaptation means that we integrate new cultural patterns into how we think and act. The fact that we adapt our behavior, however, doesn't automatically mean that we have accepted the validity of cultural difference. Let's take a closer look at how each of these reactions plays out in real life. To help you visualize this process, see figure 8.1.

RESISTANCE

People seldom talk about how intercultural experiences can reinforce negative attitudes. Talking to sojourners you may hear, "Well, I learned that you can't trust the tour guides," or "I learned that I am lucky that I was born here." Plenty of expatriates regularly run down the country they are living in. Often this takes the form of "horror stories" or "tales of my travails." These accounts seem designed to show how the sojourner has suffered at the hands of the bizarre or unreasonable behavior of the locals. Listen carefully to sojourners' descriptions of their experiences and you will regularly hear negative judgments that contain a cultural critique.

Resistance is a form of cultural denigration. Under its influence, cultural difference is perceived as representing some broader inadequacy. It can be in reaction to surface experiences ("The streets are dirty and the food was greasy") or deeper ones ("The local staff has been brainwashed to just follow orders"). Resistance seems to be a mechanism of psychological protection. If I condemn the differences I find, I can insulate myself from the need to change and learn. I can reinforce my worldview and my self-importance. I attempt to negate the subversive idea that what I find abroad is, in fact, normal.

Not all negative reactions to cultural difference constitute resistance. Sometimes we simply dislike what we find without passing judgment. I may not like eating curry with my fingers, yet I attach no negative judgment to the fact that the people around me do so. At other times we are more condemnatory. We find locals inefficient, dishonest, ignorant, and so on. The former reactions I simply call dislike, reserving the word resistance for the latter.

A sojourner who reacts with dislike takes responsibility for his or her negative reaction. You may hear, "Well, the food there was too spicy for my taste. I'm just not used to that stuff." A sojourner who expresses resistance on the other hand, finds fault with the object or experience that provoked the reactions. "You can't get any good food in that country." In other words, blame is placed outside of oneself and judgment is passed.

Sometimes we find that behavior in another place offends our personal ethical standards. This may be related to what seem to be immoral social practices, differences in gender roles, social inequality, ethnic or racial prejudice, and so on. This can lead to feelings of condemnation toward a whole community. But I believe it's possible to disagree with practices we find objectionable, keep our moral compass, and also maintain an attitude of openness and understanding.

At the other extreme, some people experience *reversal*—they find that they like their host community more than their original home. Thus, they may have a strong desire to adapt to their new home even as they denigrate their original home. Reversal may allow someone to function well in a new environment, but their intercultural sensitivity will still be limited. They have simply transferred their resistance of cultural difference from their host community to their original community. Figure 8.2 can help you visualize this reaction.

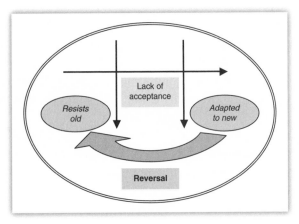

FIGURE 8.2   Reversal

Resistance is an unavoidable outcome of the psychological stresses of cultural learning. But making progress toward intercultural sensitivity requires that we set aside our judgments. We are under no obligation to like everything we experience, but we need to recognize that our discomfort often doesn't come from there being something inherently wrong with our new environment. It doesn't help to insist that things should be different simply because we're not comfortable with things as they are.

ACCEPTANCE

Some people show a lot of *acceptance*, the ability to experience cultural difference—even unpleasant difference—without feeling the need to stand in judgment or find fault. They have a fundamental recognition that one's tastes and habits are conditioned by one's background—what's not normal for me may be normal for others. Sojourners who react with acceptance often make statements about local standards that qualify their personal reactions, such as, "Well, the food was too spicy for me, but everybody eats it there," or, "They really respect authority there, so I had to change my management style."

Acceptance is perhaps the most challenging and important quality that deep culture learners need to cultivate. Coming to a deeper understanding of other cultural worlds requires a fundamental assumption that the differences we experience represent a different standard of normal, and as such deserve the openness necessary to fully understand it. This doesn't mean, of course, that we have no right to feel offended or upset at what happens to us. Individuals in the host community may try to take advantage of us or be genuinely aggressive. I'm not implying that we meekly go along with any and all demands that are made of us abroad. We do, however, need to understand how people's behavior compares to local standards.

It's often difficult to know whether how we are treated is in accord with reasonable behavior as seen by locals. Is it common for a waiter not to smile when serving food? Is the price I was quoted typical or inflated? Is this person attempting to hug me because everyone does that here? Does silence mean anger, or is this person simply thinking things through? Acceptance gives us the patience to spend the time to figure things out, defending ourselves if we must, but remaining open to learning about ourselves and our new environment.

Accepting cultural difference does not mean agreeing with all the social practices or cultural values that we encounter. I don't believe it requires us to compromise our moral or ethical standards. A Saudi immigrant to the United States told me that he found American sexual standards immoral, destructive, and disrespectful of women. But he went on to say that he understands that Americans have a very different background from his, and that he has learned to be careful not to judge particular Americans as immoral when they are simply following conventions that they find normal. He went on to say that he hopes that Westerners take the time to understand the strengths of Saudi values without passing hasty judgment on Saudi society or individual behavior.

Keeping our moral or ethical compass in a new cultural environment can be difficult. What is perceived as fair or moral is closely related to the deep cultural patterns we grow up with. Should you, for example, bribe local officials to get a contract simply because "That's the way things are done here"? There is some danger of falling into extreme cultural relativism—the belief that all social practices are acceptable simply because they represent local standards. The more subtle challenge, though, is the danger of passing judgment based on cultural assumptions that we are not aware of. Our condemnation may be too sweeping or generalized ("People are oppressed," "That society is corrupt," "They don't respect women"). Deep culture learners have a fine line to walk between accepting that there are many standards of normal at work around the world, and being true to personal feelings of right and wrong that may be evolving with ongoing experience.

ADAPTATION

We cannot remain unaffected by cultural experiences. Our cognitive unconscious autopilot is continually reading and reacting to our environment. We are so finely tuned to our surroundings that we can't help but respond. While resistance involves an attempt to maintain an internal status quo (a desire not to change), *adaptation* involves changing something about ourselves to be in closer alignment with our new environment. We may eat new food, dress differently, learn a new language, show our feelings more openly, or take on a different persona. Adaptation makes us more functional in a new place and can be as simple as learning to use a subway system or as deep as becoming bicultural.

Surface adaptation involves change to our behavior that is more explicit. If someone says, "I know all the best restaurants in Bangkok," we know they've adapted to local food. If they say, "Learning the language has really helped me feel like I belong there," we can guess that they've gone through a process of *deep adaptation*—changing more implicit parts of themselves to better function in their host environment.

Deep adaptation experiences don't happen overnight and usually involve learning a local language, forming deeper personal relations with hosts, and getting things done without depending on the special status of being a tourist or high-status expat. When this process continues long enough, it may lead to biculturalism or questions of where home is. People who've adapted deeply often have reverse culture shock when they return home.

Sometimes we're forced to adapt—think of immigrants who must learn a language or take an unpleasant job out of economic necessity. *Forced adaptation* is psychologically difficult (see figure 8.3). It may push us into insulated expatriate or immigrant communities or make us bitter toward the host community. I've seen highly privileged expatriates embittered by their cultural isolation in a country whose values they can't accept—all because they don't want to give up the high-status, high-income lifestyle they've found there. This unhealthy state is a result of two competing reactions to the stresses of being in a new place: adapting in order to function, while resisting the changes that we ourselves are making.

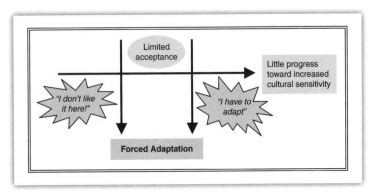

FIGURE 8.3　Forced adaptation

Adapting is not automatically good for its own sake. For it to help us develop cultural empathy, it must be accompanied by the nonjudgmental posture of acceptance. And what if the demands of a new environment are inherently unfair? This certainly happens, as when immigrants are forced to put up with racism or prejudice to keep their jobs. In this case, healthy adaptation is difficult at best. Oppressed minorities are sometimes forced to put up with degrading treatment just to survive in the dominant cultural community. This naturally creates resentment and often a powerful form of resistance.

For most of us though, the adaptive demands we most often face are value neutral. We may even find that our sense of what is right or fair evolves with our intercultural experiences. For example, my feelings about gender roles changed after having a relationship with a Mexican woman. I started to have a more nuanced view of Mexican *machismo*—something I had resisted at the beginning of my stay. This experience taught me to be more careful—not to jump too quickly to the conclusion that there's something systematically wrong with values and behavior of the people in my new home.

My discrete explanations of resistance, acceptance, and adaptation may give the impression that they exist in isolation. But we all have *mixed reactions* (a combination of different and even contradictory reactions) to adaptive demands (see figure 8.4). I remember hearing, "I love France. It's the French that I can't stand!" This was meant as a joke, but we can see the surface adaptation ("I enjoy French food and love the Musee d'Orsay") mixed with deep resistance ("French communication styles and values bother me"). Deep culture learning is a whole-body experience that goes on at many different levels.

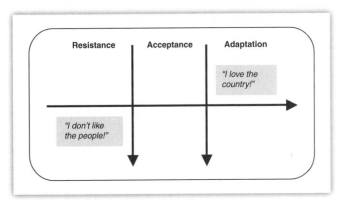

FIGURE 8.4 Mixed reactions

Our reactions to adaptive demands change as time goes by. What we resisted at the beginning of our stay may start to seem normal. We may adapt our behavior for purely practical reasons and find that over time our feelings change, too. In Japan, I resisted the practice of socializing with colleagues after working hours. It seemed an imposition of my work life onto my private time. But gradually, it started to seem normal to me and eventually I learned to enjoy it. These changes happen as we resolve feelings of resistance and integrate changes into different levels of our self.

DEEP ADAPTATION AND IDENTITY

Adapting deeply to another culture often raises identity questions such as: Where do I belong? Who and what am I loyal to? Where is home? People living abroad also face concrete questions about whom to marry, where to live, how to raise children, what language to speak at home, and so on. If you face these questions, here are a few things to keep in mind.

Cultural learning is additive. Just as you never forget your native language, you will always have within you the patterns of your original cultural community (since you understand it from the inside). That doesn't mean, of course, that you will feel that you belong there. And if you were raised in more than one cultural community, you may be in a position of never having felt fully at home anywhere.

Cultural understanding and cultural identity are different things. Having an insider's view doesn't automatically make you feel a sense of belonging or loyalty. And not having an insider's view doesn't prevent you from joining a cultural community. I myself feel very much at home in Japan, though I will never be seen as Japanese by the people that live there.

Resolving feelings of cultural marginality requires forming relationships. We don't form an identity around culture but through our connection to individuals who form part of a greater community. And belonging doesn't require a specific geographic home. You can feel deeply connected to people who share your values or lifestyle, even if they speak different languages or live far away. If you can't find a ready-made community that you fit into, you can create one of your own. I, for instance, have friends that I may see only once every year or two, but we remain a source of support and stability for each other because we share things that are important to us.

DEEP CULTURE LEARNING AND SELF-AWARENESS

I've suggested that you listen to the accounts of travelers to develop a sense for the three fundamental responses to cultural learning: resistance, acceptance, and adaptation.

Of course, the larger goal is to become more aware of this process in oneself. Doing so makes it easier to let go of resistance and engage more fully with our cultural learning. Acceptance is the key ingredient to the deeper learning that travel can bring. Ultimately, we have only two options: retreat into the defense of the existing self or openness to the transformational possibilities to be found in meeting adaptive challenges.

But cultural learning involves more than a need for personal flexibility. We also face the challenge of making sense of the cultural differences we find in our new environment. Learning to make sense of people's behavior (instead of finding it arbitrary or ill willed) helps us let go of resistance. It's often not easy to figure out how to get things done, learn to read people, and decipher the way that people think. Looking beneath the surface applies not only to a need to look within oneself, it also means finding hidden cultural patterns in the behavior of others. The next chapter gives some pointers for doing this.

CHAPTER NINE

Understanding Cultural Difference

PHILIPPE, A FRENCH RESEARCHER LIVING in Germany, recounted to me how a German neighbor knocked on his door to remind him to separate his garbage properly. Philippe admitted that he hadn't paid much attention to the rules, but he was taken aback that his neighbor had noticed and had gone so far as to come and talk to him about it. Philippe concluded by saying that as much as he liked German efficiency, he couldn't stand what he felt to be extreme pickiness about rules and regulations. "*C'est pas normal*," he said—it's just not normal.

For the deep culture learner, trying to figure out what's normal is a continual challenge. The behavior of our cultural hosts may not make sense to us. Their priorities may seem misplaced. We may have trouble reading their intentions. There may be cultural assumption or expectations that we haven't noticed. We may be surprised, as Philippe was, by the strength of the reactions that our behavior provokes. This may offend our sense of what's reasonable or fair.

Sojourners who plan to spend time in a foreign country often want to know what cultural differences they will find while there. What customs or etiquette must they know to get along? Some basic knowledge is very useful—such as knowing not to pass food from chopsticks to chopsticks in Japan (it recalls a funeral ceremony). But as Philippe discovered, the more challenging elements of cultural difference are beneath the surface and hard to explain. Just what is this difference between French and German attitudes toward rules and regulations?

There are plenty of people who feel that trying to generalize about cultural differences is nearly impossible. So much of behavior is situational, or depends on the person, that there's a danger of simply spouting stereotypes. Rather than pointing out supposed differences, the argument goes, we should focus on what we have in common—our fundamental humanity. This is the message of the "It's a Small World" attraction at Disneyland.

Someone who advocates this approach might say that Philippe's problem is that he is taking cultural difference too seriously. Philippe and the neighbor should both lighten up. The problem isn't so much cultural difference as human nature.

It's true that people everywhere share a common human nature. We all laugh and cry, want to protect loved ones, look for meaning in our lives, and so on. But cultural programming is also part of human nature. Philippe's definition of what was normal didn't include German intuitions about rules and systems. What we think is simply human nature may be strongly flavored by cultural assumptions.

Beware of those who insist too vehemently that they can get along with anyone in any country by simply being themselves. They will argue that "people are just people," but that's like a husband who says, "I understand my wife because I know how women think." Understanding a particular individual, or a specific cultural community, requires more than a set of universal principles. Still, it can be valuable to see what we can be sure to find no matter where we go.

SIMPLE UNIVERSALS

The elements that are universal to all human societies are sometimes easy to spot. People everywhere love their children, for example, and understand basic facial expressions such as happiness, sadness, surprise, disgust, fear, and anger. Specialists have created long lists of such universals, such as gossip; lying; verbal humor; words for past, present, and future; giving; lending; kinship categories; crying; expressions of affection; sexual jealousy; adornment; fear of snakes; use of tools; drugs; shelter; status and prestige; gender distinctions; sanctions against violence, rape, and murder; a sense of etiquette; mourning the dead; and a taste for sweets!

But lists like this can be misleading. These *simple universals* are only marginally helpful when we experience cultural difference because they tell us the *what* but not the *how* of life in another place. For example, all societies make gender distinctions, but how much affection couples show in public varies widely. Adornment and status markers are cultural universals, but the specific meaning of tattoos and neckties varies. The devil is in the details.

This doesn't mean, of course, that on our sojourns we can't have meaningful interactions based on our common humanity. People in many places often don't expect foreigners to observe local custom, and a smile really can go a long way when we are abroad. And we should be ourselves, without obsessing over local norms. But this basic interaction is just the starting point. As we involve ourselves more with a host community, we have a lot to gain by exploring cultural difference.

ASKING WHY

Philippe's reaction to his (helpful? nosy?) neighbor is understandable. Yet he seems to be missing a larger point. When he says that German attitudes toward rules are "not normal," he is saying that they don't make sense—they are extreme or arbitrary. But this isn't true. They do make sense and they are quite normal, if you've grown up in Germany and are used to doing things that way. Philippe is running into a different "common sense" about the relative importance of rules and systems. The regulations for separating garbage are on the surface of the cultural onion and are indicative of deeper values and assumptions.

In chapter 2, we saw that we can attempt to understand the hidden norms, values, and assumptions that underlie behavior by asking, "Why?" If we ask a German why it's important to follow the rules about separating garbage, she might say that it's simply the way things are done (a norm), or because the rules were made to facilitate the garbage treatment process (the value of efficiency), and that they also should be followed because they serve everyone (the value of fairness). Underlying these values are the even more hidden assumptions that efficiency and fairness are well served by a depersonalized and systematic approach to problems.

The differences we find in simple behaviors like separating garbage have roots in more fundamental questions of social organization. The way a community thinks about rules is a tool of social cohesion—it helps people get along based on shared standards for how to approach problems.

Looked at in this way, cultural difference is not infinite. It revolves around the challenges that human communities face when trying to organize themselves and collaborate. These deeper patterns, if understood, can help us make sense of some of the more hidden elements of cultural difference we encounter during our sojourns.

UNIVERSAL DILEMMAS

One influential approach to understanding these deeper patterns of cultural difference was developed by anthropologist Clyde Kluckhohn. He argued that cultural difference can be understood as value orientations toward key elements of human life, such as human nature, time, and social relations.[1] These orientations can be described in terms of differing assumptions. Does, for example, a cultural community assume that human nature is, for example, fundamentally good or evil?

Using this approach as a starting point, the intercultural management specialists Trompenaars and Hampden-Turner have described cultural value orientations as a set of universal dilemmas. Their approach revolves around things such as the role of the individual versus the group, how social systems can best ensure fairness, expectations about status, ways to divide up our life spaces, assumptions about fate and control, and how we conceptualize time.[2]

These orientations are referred to as *dilemmas* because they involve fundamentally contradictory elements of the human experience that must be reconciled for people to get along. For example, humans have individual identities and desires yet must also live in groups to survive. This creates a built-in tension between the more generalized collective need of the group and the more specific desires of its individual members. In families, for example, we will always find children who go against the wishes of other family members. In any group, there will always be members who stand out, don't fit in, or can't get along. If this tension isn't resolved constructively, the group becomes dysfunctional.

This dilemma-based thinking about culture assumes that there is more than one possible solution to dilemmas like these. In the case of the individual and the group, we can resolve it by charging all members of the group with responsibility for the individual well-being of each member. Therefore, the collective is responsible for each individual member. We can also resolve it by assuming that the individual is primarily responsible for herself, and that having attained individual well-being, she is responsible for contributing to the well-being of the larger group.

These are more than mere abstractions. Whole societies are built up on these assumptions, often tending more toward one assumption or the other. The individualism of the United States is deeply rooted in the ideal of individual autonomy and a deep distrust of the collective. The ideals of *solidarité* and *fraternité* in France, for example, emphasize the idea that the collective is responsible for protecting the rights of the individual. In Muslim societies, individuals are seen as part of a larger organic whole, just as the hand is part of the body.

With this general approach in mind, I have listed some questions that we can ask ourselves when trying to understand the cultural differences we find abroad. They are based on the value-orientation understanding of culture that I've referred to previously. They have helped me make sense of much of the cultural difference that I have experienced. I use them to make observations and better understand my own reactions to the cultural differences I find.

Yet there are some important caveats. First, I am not saying that people from a given community all act or think in the same way. How people act depends on much more than cultural orientations. The goal is not to predict how people will act or define them with overly simplistic labels. We are simply looking at cultural intuitions—differing ways that people make sense of some of the important choices in their lives. And when trying to interpret the behavior of individuals, remember: the people in a given community who are most friendly to outsiders are often those who are less representative of the larger group.

Whom are people loyal to?

Perhaps the most important universal dilemma revolves around the dilemma I've already mentioned—an individual's relationship to others in his or her community. Ask Americans who they are loyal to and they will often say, "Myself," or "My beliefs." In China, you will find a powerful loyalty to family. In Afghanistan, you may be loyal to your fellow Pashtuns, Uzbeks, or Turkmen. This distinction between an emphasis on one's personal priorities and an emphasis on the larger community is sometimes referred to as *individualism* versus *collectivism*.

Loyalty is closely tied to responsibility. We are loyal to those who we feel have our best interests in mind. In a more individualist community, individual responsibility is emphasized. We find this ideal in the English expression, "God helps those who help themselves." In more collectivist communities, one's responsibility to the family, religious group, or tribe is felt strongly. And while someone with a more individualistic orientation may feel that loyalty to a group suppresses individual freedom, those in a more collectivist community will see the individual as developed *in the context of* the collective. They believe we develop our unique abilities thanks to the support of those in our family, church, or community.

Would you go against your family's wishes to satisfy your personal aspirations? If so, you may explain your decision using an individualist's logic. If not, you may explain it with a more collectivist one. If people seem egocentric and self-centered when you are abroad, it may be because you don't understand their individualist values. If they seem overly dependent on their family, tribe, or religious community, remember that these communities nurture them as individuals.

Who gets respect?

Status markers are another human universal. In every community, some people are marked as deserving special attention or consideration. Yet the kinds of things that are valued vary in systematic ways. One example is the difference between an emphasis on *achieved status* (based on actions or performance) and *ascribed status* (official status based on titles, age, diplomas, and so on). Achieved status is related to *doing*—being the best player, highest earner, and so on. Ascribed status is related to *being*—having a certain age, holding a particular rank, or being the holder of a special degree or certification.

The United States is often held up as an example of a society that values achievement and distrusts ascribed rank and titles. In a job interview, the prospective employee will hear, "Tell me what you can do." In France, holding a degree from an elite educational institution marks you as an elite individual for life. In Japan, employers often want to see formally recognized evidence of achievement, such as a particular score on a Test of English as a Foreign Language (TOEFL). It's not enough to *say* that you can speak English; you need to prove yourself using a standard that is formally recognized.

For people who come from communities that emphasize achieved status, it will make sense to answer the question, "Whom do you respect?" by saying, "People who can do something well." In communities in which ascribed status is emphasized, it will make sense to answer "Elders," "The boss," or more generally, people who have gotten a particular degree, certificate, or rank.

If your deep culture settings orient you toward achieved status, you may find people in some places too hung up on titles, formality, or etiquette. Remember that these status markers act not only as rewards but as standards that people live up to. If your deep culture settings orient you toward ascribed status, you may find people in some places to be overly confident self-promoters. Remember that in such communities people act that way so to be taken seriously.

How do we ensure fairness and efficiency?

We've seen that Philippe found German rules for separating garbage to be excessive. Fairness and efficiency require predictability (everyone follows the same rules) and flexibility (sometimes exceptions must be made). Some communities, such as Germany, emphasize *universalism* (an emphasis on systems and rules), while others, in this case France, *particularism* (a case-by-case approach).

One way to get an intuitive sense for this difference is to consider how much we trust or rely on systems and procedures to provide equality, fairness, and efficiency. A universalistic logic assumes, like Philippe's neighbor, that rules work in everyone's favor. The particularist logic found in France finds systematic thinking to be impersonal and dehumanizing. If a Swiss pedestrian waits for the green light to cross the street even though there are no cars coming, he would probably justify it with a universalistic logic that rules should be followed for the good of everyone. If an Italian pedestrian crosses in the same situation, she may explain it using the particularist logic that every situation requires prudent judgment by the individual, not simply a blind adherence to impersonal standards. An Italian in Switzerland may find Zurich efficient yet overly organized and sterile. A Swiss in Italy may find Rome charming but chaotic.

How should we manage our emotions?

On the one hand, human emotion must be controlled to prevent unnecessary conflict. On the other, human emotion must be expressed to allow for open relationships. These two truisms represent the opposing poles of a *neutral* approach to feelings and an *expressive* one. The neutral approach guards against excesses of emotion, while the expressive one sees emotion as fundamentally healthy. While living in Mexico, I was told that Americans are like machines—they lack human warmth and feeling. When I went to Japan, I was told that Americans are very friendly and expressive.

These differences don't mean that emotion is expressed more in Mexico than in Japan. Japanese are just as effective at reading each other's emotional states as Mexicans are theirs. Japanese are more attuned to subtle signs of feeling—they learn to have a very sensitive emotional radar. This means that when interacting with people from more emotive cultures, they may feel overwhelmed by loud voices, embraces, physical contact, open sadness and anger, and so on. A Saudi used to his country's emotive behavior may find

Finnish people (whose behavior is often more emotionally neutral) to be cold or impersonal.

So if you get the impression that people abroad are hiding behind a mask of self-control, remind yourself that their feelings are expressed in more subtle ways. You can usually count on them to read your emotional cues quite carefully, and they probably won't need you to raise your voice or exhibit your emotions in obvious ways. If people seem to you overly emotional, expressive, or aggressive, remind yourself that a raised voice or expansive gestures don't necessarily signify extreme emotion. These differences can be hard to get used to, since we experience emotion at such a visceral level. But dealing with them can help expand our communication repertoire, helping us to be both more sensitive and more expressive.

Who's in control?

In Muslim communities, when you say, "See you tomorrow!" in anticipation of an appointment, you may hear the reply *inshallah* or literally, "If Allah wills it." This expression is more than a turn of phrase. It reflects the deep culture assumption that humans are not ultimately in control of their fate. Communities that emphasize the importance of destiny, magic, and adapting to circumstance share a similar orientation toward *outer control*.

This kind of thinking may strike Americans or Western Europeans as superstitious or passive. Their deep culture assumption of *inner control* emphasizes humans as agents of their own development and change. This can create the impression of egocentrism or godlessness for those oriented more toward *outer control*. Who can presume, after all, to know the future or to control the larger forces that govern our lives?

Asian companies are known for being highly sensitive to the needs of their customers and markets. This reflects an orientation toward outer control, as do martial arts like Ju-jitsu, which focus on using the strength of one's opponent to one's own advantage. The Western concern for invention and originality reflects the inner control assumption that true creativity is something that comes from within, not as an adaptation or modification of something without.

What time is it?

Why do people from some communities seem so unconcerned with precise scheduling? Why do others let themselves become slaves to the clock and their day planners?

Time can be conceived of as *absolute*—an objective part of physical reality. This implies that humans should use it as any other limited resource (in English we *spend*, *waste*, and *give of* our time). In other words, its use should be as predictable as possible (to avoid wasting it!). But time can also be thought of as *situational*, with important events and people allotted more time as circumstances dictate. If something comes up and we don't finish everything today, there's always tomorrow.

On one occasion in Mexico, I was walking down the street on my way to meet my girlfriend. I ran into a friend on the sidewalk and stopped to talk. My friend had just bought a new car and went on at length about it, until I started to feel uncomfortable, knowing that this conversation was making me late. After a few more minutes, I motioned toward my wristwatch and apologetically said, "Sorry, but I'm afraid I have an appointment that I'm late for." My friend looked slightly taken aback and retorted, "You're so American. The machine on your wrist is more important to you than your friend in front of your eyes."

The logic of situational time is that time is allotted based what's important to us. What I should have done, of course, was motion in the direction of my waiting girlfriend and explain, "Sorry, I'm afraid my girlfriend is waiting for me, and I really don't want to keep her waiting." This would have alerted my friend to the important person who was, in effect, competing for my time at that moment.

People who are used to absolute time tend to assume that dividing time into small increments and making behavior subservient to them (for example, "Let's try and get this done by five") is automatically more efficient. But this is only true when dealing with tasks that can be predictably organized in this way. It's certainly true when running a factory. But a farmer, artist, or software developer needs flexibility to organize her time around the needs of the harvest, the artwork, or the project. In my case, I learned a lot from being with people who are not upset by minor delays or events that aren't predictable. When I find myself irritated because the adjacent line at the supermarket is moving a bit faster than mine, I feel that I have allowed absolute time to dominate my perception of the situation.

For sojourners, these differing attitudes can lead toward the impression of chronic tardiness, on the one hand, or planning and interacting, on the other. If you have the former impression when you travel, don't waste your emotional energy resenting meetings that start late or people who don't arrive when you expect. Learn local expectations and take advantage of the spare moments they create. And if you find that everyone is rushed and obsessed with scheduling, remember that in some places predictability is sacred and that sometimes (in business, for example) squeezing activities carefully into a limited time frame can be advantageous for everyone.

How can we judge goodness and truth?

If you disappoint people who are dear to you, do you feel guilty or ashamed? Guilt comes from having an *inner reference* for truth and goodness—we look inside ourselves to our conscience; our connection with our God, and our ideals. Shame comes from an *outer reference*—we judge our behavior by looking outside ourselves, focusing on the relationships we are in and our influence on others.

Christianity, Islam, and Judaism share a deep culture orientation toward inner referencing. Parents scold their children by saying, "You *know* better than that," hoping to develop this inner voice of their conscience. One's internal beliefs or principles are seen as a defining characteristic of who you are. U.S. Americans often feel that having no clear belief is worse than having a wrong belief. People who have no clear beliefs are seen as lacking a moral compass.

In Asia, children may be told, "You're bothering people!" by parents who hope to develop an outer-referenced sense of responsibility to others. Confucian thinking emphasizes the importance of the social roles that we play—being a good son, father, leader, and so on. A moral person is one who can live up to the responsibilities built into these relationships, regardless of possible inner grumbling. In Japan, people are all assumed to have a *honne* (true inner feelings), which they may need to set aside for the sake of the greater good. Acting in accordance with social expectations, or *tatemae*, is not dishonest; it simply recognizes that, regardless of private feelings, our behavior has an important impact on others.

Inner-referenced thinking is not only associated with individualistic thinking. Arab communities, for example, are influenced by the inner referenced thinking of personal faith found in Islam, yet also have strongly collectivist expectations towards the family and one's religious community. One is expected to live up to one's personal moral responsibilities in public so as not to set a bad example and bring communal shame onto your family, faith, and so on. One's inner moral state is seen as exerting an important influence over those in the community. Thus, community standards should reflect, as much as possible, these moral ideals. In more inner-referenced communities, such as the Netherlands, personal morality is largely seen as best left up to the individual.

How different are men and women?

Men and women are different—that's true. Men and women are similar—that's also true. Communities tend to intuit one of these ideas as a starting point for an understanding of what it means to be feminine or masculine. A *gender-separate* approach assumes that differing gender roles are a natural outgrowth of fundamental differences between men and women. It claims that biology dictates a large portion of what we are. A *gender-similar* orientation starts with the idea that men and women are more fundamentally the same. Biological differences are considered secondary.

If you go abroad and think that gender relations are oppressive and patriarchal, remember that not everything can be reduced to power relations. People often thrive in their gender-based roles of mother, father, protector, nurturer, provider, and so on. Many good things come from gender role specialization. As one female visitor to the United States said, "But I don't *want* to be like a man."

If, on the other hand, you go abroad and feel that men are weak and women are pushy, or that the value of family, modesty, or honor is not respected, remember the great variety between men and between women. Treating the genders as though they were the same can allow for otherwise hidden abilities to flourish. Swedish children whose fathers get paternity leave from work certainly benefit from the time with their fathers.

Am I in your space?

Humans are territorial, like our primate ancestors and the mammals we evolved from. As humans started living in larger groups, we had to carve our spaces into ever more complicated units. Some communities emphasize *discrete space*, with clear delineation between the different parts of one's life. If you run into a friend from school while you are out with colleagues, would you invite the friend to join you? If not, you are marking clear boundaries between life spaces. Others emphasize *diffuse space*, with porous boundaries between the different compartments of our lives—a friend of a friend is my friend.

These boundaries help us define our *private space*—the physical and psychological spaces that only people we are close to have access to. *Public space* belongs to those we have no special obligations to. In communities with a larger public space, people will strike up conversations with strangers in elevators or bus stops. Communities with a strong sense of private space erect clear boundaries to protect inner sanctums from outsiders. The high walls, restricted areas, and inner gardens of traditional Arab architecture contrasts with the "Let me show you around the house" of Americans who even give a tour to casual guests.

Relationships can be discrete or diffuse as well. In Latin America, if you happen to meet your boss on the tennis court, you still defer to her. In the United States, relationships tend to be more discrete, with different life spaces each calling for separate relationships—you are free to defeat your boss on the golf course! The boundaries between thinking and feeling can be more or less discrete or diffuse as well. For a Brazilian, exchanging ideas with a German collaborator can be rather brutal because the German will assume that it's only the *ideas* that are being criticized. In Latin America, if you criticize ideas, you are criticizing the person who came up with the ideas as well.

These differing ways of dividing up life spaces can lead to quite complex combinations. Germans and Japanese (small public space) may agree that Americans are overly friendly (large public space). Japanese tend to have diffuse relationships (your boss is always your boss), yet divide their private life spaces into very distinct areas (different categories of friends, seldom inviting the boss to your home). Arabs and Japanese both distinguish clearly between public and private. Yet among Arabs private spaces are quite diffuse (friends and family form part of a diffuse network), while in Japan private spaces are quite discrete. In intercultural settings, it can take a lot of trial and error interaction to work out the particular makeup of the life spaces of the people you are dealing with.

Shall we look forward or back?

Making effective choices in life requires reliance on past experience. Yet that which worked before may not be an effective guide for the future. A *past orientation* implies a trust for using what has come before to reference what is to come. In Muslim societies, for example, the Koran represents valuable lessons from the past that can be applied to modern life. A *future orientation*, on the other hand, assumes more often that the past is a hindrance that can impede the good things assumed to be ahead. American society's emphasis on "progress" is an example of this. This can be contrasted with the caution that new technology is treated with in a country such as Bhutan.

A future orientation can be found in advertising which emphasizes "new and improved" or a concern for the "latest thing." In contrast, the brand of hot chocolate I used to buy in Mexico was called *Abuelita* (Grandma). It was packaged and advertised to suggest past-oriented authenticity. How, after all, could you ever improve on the hot chocolate that Grandma used to make?

If you find people in your travels who seem to be stuck in traditional thinking that impedes progress, remind yourself that change is not good for its own sake, and that new doesn't always mean improved. And if you find that people are throwing away the valuable lessons of previous generations, remind yourself that even the oldest traditions were at one time new, and that change can lead to a rediscovery of values of the past.

THE PITFALLS OF LABELING

The use of categories like these to describe cultural difference is sometimes criticized as reductionist or stereotypical. In my mind, however, this terminology can act as a good starting point for looking beneath the surface of our experiences. Don't be fooled by the brevity of these explanations. The hidden differences that these questions point to are simple but deep. Understanding them as ideas is easy, but it can take years of living in a given community to integrate new ways of thinking and experiencing into your behavior and sense of self. After living in Mexico for three years, I still had trouble fully entering into the subtleties and efficiencies of how people experienced time, related to their families, or showed emotion. Living in Japan, it took years to internalize the different sense of public versus private space, or the outer-referenced emphasis of being aware of the effects of one's behavior on others.

Some people talk about the influence of culture as though it were a sort of operant conditioning—a set of automatic responses that we have learned. Sometimes that's true. If you grow up in a community with taboos about eating a certain food, the thought of eating it can generate genuine disgust. Yet while our community certainly does train us to react to certain things in certain ways, deep culture is not simply an internalized series of responses. As I've tried to show with the questions in this chapter, deep culture relates to how we make sense of things, rather than simply affective responses to particular phenomena.

It can be difficult to talk about cultural difference in neutral terms. One pitfall is that the words used to talk about culture would be better suited to talking about the personalities of individuals. For example, you might hear that Japanese are "shy," or that Americans are "friendly," yet a whole nation of people cannot all be shy or friendly. These words refer to a way of acting compared to some assumed standard of normal. Someone we say is shy falls short in some way. In addition, personality words often have positive or negative connotations. Most of us would rather be described as friendly than shy.

In that sense, the categories listed in this chapter can help us. Rather than saying that Italians are "passionate," we can say that the communication style of our guide in Italy was very expressive. Yet be careful when applying these categories to people. They do not represent some kind of essence that controls behavior or defines identity. We all apply both sides of these cultural logics in our lives and in our societies. There are plenty of Germans who can't stand rules and regulations, or Italians who wait at red lights even when there is no traffic. It's easy to overgeneralize when using these labels, and it's safer to use these categories to make sense of things rather than to define people or countries.

Understanding cultural difference requires much more than an intellectual understanding of customs or even these deeper cultural logics. It is, in the end, an intuitive process based on trial and error. My hope is that by having these intellectual tools at our disposal, we can better suspend judgment and thus find deeper patterns that we might miss otherwise. If Philippe gave his interaction with his neighbor a bit more thought, he may have better understood that his experiences in Germany could teach him about his own deep culture programming.

CHAPTER TEN

Deep Culture,
Clash,
and
Cash

A SOJOURN ABROAD CAN BRING YOU face to face with horrifying gaps between rich and poor. A child born into a typical family in Haiti faces very different prospects from one raised in Switzerland. Things that are taken for granted in the latter (like clean water, adequate shelter, social services, job opportunities, health care, and schools) are often in short supply in the former. And these disparities are present on every continent, often within a single country. It's like a worldwide quality-of-life lottery with a few big winners and lots of losers.

Experienced up close, these disparities are gut-wrenching. While traveling I have spent as much for a single meal as would feed a poor family for a month. I have seen beggars, shanty towns, and children playing in garbage while their parents scavenged in sewage. These experiences can provoke a feeling of helplessness, since it's not clear how to solve these problems. In spite of worldwide technological progress and years of development aid, there are many places in the world that remain in dire straits. And even when economic development is achieved, it can bring with it terrible environmental destruction.

There are other hard realities that can't be avoided if you spend time in different places around the world. There's no shortage of prejudice and ethnocentrism—it often seems the rule rather than the exception. Every community has negative stereotypes about somebody. I have been the target of aggression because of my national origin. A mixed-race couple I knew had their honeymoon abroad ruined by racial slurs and insults as they walked on the streets of a country they were visiting for the first time. Ethnic tensions live on in many places. Oppression, violence, and even genocide based on national origin, ethnicity, or religious affiliation have not died out as a result of globalization. In some places, the history of violence between neighboring communities goes back for generations, with little sign of stopping.

The issue of culture often comes up in discussions of these issues. We hear terms like a *culture of poverty* or *culture of war*. Cultural and ethnic pride can turn into intolerance toward outsiders. Development specialists remind us that aid projects must take local culture into account. Traditional cultural beliefs and practices may include destructive environmental practices or resistance to new technologies. And sometimes cultural values (such as an emphasis on education) are used to explain economic development (or lack thereof).

So are these problems, at least in part, cultural?

I would have liked to avoid bringing up such a broad and contentious subject. After all, this book focuses on what we can learn from intercultural experiences, not social and economic issues. But I believe that deep culture learners shouldn't shy away from such important topics. We needn't stick to feel-good declarations about cultural diversity and tolerance. We hope that our experiences around the world and a deeper understanding of culture can inform our approach to solving these global challenges.

So let's take just a brief look at the intersection of culture, conflict, and economic development. While a deeper understanding of culture won't solve all these problems, it can act as important background knowledge when looking for possible answers.

CLASH

In 1993, political scientist Samuel Huntington published an article in the influential journal *Foreign Affairs* titled "The Clash of Civilizations?" His article, and the book he published to elaborate on his ideas, ignited a firestorm of controversy about how best to understand the causes of conflict in our modern era.[1]

Huntington's main idea is that much of today's geopolitical friction fits historical patterns of cultural competition that are hundreds, if not thousands, of years old. He sees the world as having areas of shared cultural history, identity, and values—what he calls *civilizations*—that naturally tend to collaborate to compete for dominance with the others. He argues that political events are best understood in this context of civilizational competition.

This idea provoked intense debate, particularly in the aftermath of the terrorist attacks on September 11, 2001. For some, it provided a new way to understand the often overlooked cultural element in geopolitical events. But for others, it seemed a gross oversimplification, overly deterministic, divisive, and perhaps even discriminatory. The critics argued that such simple categories as civilizations were meaningless given the cultural diversity in any given region and the complex interrelations that characterize globalization. The idea that a war or terrorism could be explained by things that happened hundreds of years ago seemed far-fetched at best.

I hope, however, that by starting to understand deep culture, we can see that our attitudes and values, feelings of territoriality, sense of identity, and understanding of what is fair and normal in the world are all closely tied to deep culture settings that operate outside of awareness. It doesn't seem such a radical an idea that the countries of Western Europe share deep culture settings, just as Slavic or East Asian countries do.

And religion is more than a set of conscious beliefs or practices. Religious worldviews reflect deep culture assumptions that can unify as well as divide. And while it certainly would be an oversimplification to talk about a Christian, Muslim, or Buddhist worldview, there are deep culture differences to be found in the assumptions of different religious and philosophical traditions. Christianity is, in many ways, a religion of the individual, while Islam has a strong focus on community. Buddhism and Hinduism focus more on states of being than on actions. Animistic traditions see the material world as not-so-separate from the spiritual one. These differences are diffuse and hard to clearly define or measure precisely because they are so foundational. They can be stated only as abstractions or generalizations, but that doesn't mean they don't have a powerful influence on how people view the world or live their lives—whether they consider themselves practitioners or not.

CULTURAL CONFLICT AND DIFFERENT REALITIES

In an experiment carried out by social psychologists, volunteers were told that they would be tested on their ability to use a device to pinch someone with the exact degree of force that they had been pinched with. A pinches B, then B pinches A, trying to match the strength of A's pinch. The cycle continues. So what happened? You might think that force would decrease because people wouldn't want to antagonize the other participant. In fact, the opposite happened, and each person escalated the strength of their pinches, creating a runaway tit-for-tat cycle.[2]

The reason for this happening between two well-meaning individuals is simple. Because of how our brain processes our experiences and imagines those of others, the pain that we feel is always more real to us than the pain that we inflict. Yet we tend to assume that other people can accurately gauge the suffering they inflict on us. In the research mentioned, this resulted in both participants feeling that the other person wasn't following the rules that had been laid out—that they were taking advantage of the experiment to intentionally cause pain. This led to what each person thought was justified retaliation, which then fed the vicious cycle. Both participants felt victimized and also felt justified inflicting pain.

This simple experiment illustrates a foundational insight of deep culture learning. Though we live in an objective physical world, the world of our experience (our perceptual world) is greatly affected by how our brain processes information and by the social and cultural expectations we have when interacting with others. And not only do individuals have different points of view, people in different cultural communities have different worldviews. This means that two people, or two groups of people, can witness the same event and understand it in completely different— even opposing—ways.

It's not difficult to find examples. Spousal conflict can closely resemble the patterns found in this experiment. At the macro level, we can find people on both sides of the Israeli/Palestinian conflict who feel victimized and make sense of their own role in the conflict in radically different ways. This can lead to a vicious cycle of retribution and distrust. And in a cruel twist of social logic, close contact between the two sides can breed ever more distrust, because the ongoing behavior of the other reinforces the negative conclusions that each side has.

Differing interpretations of events also point to a human tendency to assign blame for bad events based on cause-and-effect reasoning. This is natural in the context of our evolutionary heritage. Humans learned to survive in the natural world by figuring out these kinds of relationships. But the more complex phenomena of political and social conflict cannot be so easily defined in this way. There is no single "cause" for a war or aggressive act. Deep culture learning teaches us that rather than seek absolute answers, we should seek to understand as many perspectives about a problem as possible. This will allow us to construct a view of the situation that is more realistic and best explains the facts on the ground.

DEEP CULTURE VERSUS CIVILIZATION

So can we say that cultural differences are the *cause* of conflict? No. General societal attitudes, beliefs, or values don't cause things to happen. Belonging to a particular religion, ethnic group, or country does not *make* someone act in a certain way, any more than speaking a particular language makes one say particular things. Conflict is caused through an interaction of any number of factors—economic, political, and so on.

But human tendencies related to deep culture difference can contribute to war, ethnic conflict, genocide, terrorism, and so on. Deep culture functions on a gut level. This helps explain the fervor around issues of politics, religion, and war. And deep culture learning shows us that ethnocentrism encourages the perception of difference as a threat, of the "other" as strange or less than human. Broadly speaking, humans have a capacity for prejudice and dehumanization that is part of our evolutionary psychology.

When discussing culture and conflict, it's important to distinguish between ethnocentrism and learned prejudice. As previously mentioned, *ethnocentrism* is the natural tendency to see one's own cultural community as primary. It is at the base of the "us" versus "them" feeling that permeates human social interaction. *Learned prejudice*, on the other hand, is when we grow up hearing things like, "Those people are dirty."

Ethnocentrism is the psychological mechanism that is exploited by people who perpetuate prejudice. Yet both ethnocentrism and prejudice largely function out of awareness. When people spout ethnocentric or prejudicial attitudes, they themselves often feel that they are simply reporting the facts, which explains why arguing about what they say often antagonizes rather than enlightens.

Understanding factors that contribute to prejudice and conflict is not the same as excusing it. Ethnocentrism is a natural result of our evolutionary biology, but that doesn't mean that it is desirable. Nature is not destiny. Sickness and death are also a natural part of life, but understanding the body gives us choices for how to maintain our health.

Fortunately, research in recent years has provided (at least in general terms) guidance for how to move forward. For example, social psychologists have found that to reduce the tensions between groups in antagonistic relationships, simply creating opportunities for interaction and communication isn't enough. Having a superordinate goal—one that requires more than one group to achieve—is a more important reducer of intergroup tension. This is one important reason that economic interdependence reduces conflict. It's not simply that it's in people's self-interest to avoid war (human's often do things that are not in their best interest), but that interaction and institutions that require cooperation and are mutually beneficial can break down in-group/out-group barriers.

This makes sense in terms of human evolutionary biology. Humans evolved in communities that featured both *zero-sum* (win-lose) social relationships, as well as *reciprocal altruism* ("Let's help each other and all come out ahead"). Groups perceived as belonging to the former category are competitors or the "enemy." The latter are easier to perceive as deserving altruistic behavior. As societies have become larger, people have learned to feel connected to those who are farther and farther removed from their daily lives. Ten thousand years ago, few humans considered themselves connected to people who didn't live in their immediate vicinity, but today many do. Creating these connections—whether through cultural exchange, business relationships, tourism, or virtual communities—can contribute to this process. But as we've seen, having contact isn't enough. We need shared goals and a need to collaborate to achieve them. Certainly one of those shared goals can be economic development.

CASH

So what about the tremendous gap between rich and poor? There are some uncomfortable culture-related questions that come up in relation to economic development, such as: Why have some societies industrialized while others have not? Do certain cultural values or practices make economic development more difficult? Do some traditional beliefs and practices get in the way of solving these problems? How about a community in which bribery is common? How about traditional taboos that create resistance to modern health practices? How about communities where there is little traditional emphasis on saving and planning for the future?

Simply bringing up these questions can be provocative. Pointing to culture as a "problem" can seem prejudiced—a case of blaming the victim. After all, there are plenty of other places to point the finger. Powerful countries often impose their will on, and extract natural resources from, economically weaker countries (and some countries have few natural resources to begin with). Many poor countries have a history of capricious and destructive colonial rule.

Even the definition of *development* is suspect. After all, a bigger gross national product (GNP) and greater industrialization doesn't make a society superior. Societies can be rich yet have serious social problems. The country with the largest GDP in the world (the USA) has high rates of incarceration, violent crime, and divorce. Having a strong economy doesn't solve all problems. Many would go further and argue that the glorification of economic profit and personal gain reduces our quality of life by making us forget important things like family, community, and spiritual development. Does eating at McDonald's or buying the latest technological gadget make us happy?

But rather than trying to figure out who to blame, let's look at how an understanding of deep culture can help us unravel some of these issues. Let's start with Max Weber. He was the political economist who, in the late nineteenth century, first argued that there is a strong relationship between cultural values and economic systems.[3] He was particularly interested in the sociology of religion and argued that Protestant cultural values were instrumental in the development of capitalism. For a time, some argued that Western values of individualism and personal autonomy were a requirement for the development of industrialized economies. Since then there has been tremendous economic success—in East Asia and India in particular—that shows that Western values and social systems are not a prerequisite for economic development.

Despite this, many questions remain. For example, why is there such a gap between the economies of different countries and regions? Are there cultural reasons for poverty and social dysfunction? Development specialists have not been able to come up with a definitive answer. It's clear that geographic and historical factors explain many differences in economic output. Materially impoverished countries, for example, are more often landlocked, have fewer natural resources, and have a history of colonial control.

Nevertheless, years of development aid have also shown us that poverty, lack of basic social services, poorly developed health care systems, and political corruption are part of the fabric of society in many places. Simply lending technical assistance or giving money for new agricultural practices doesn't solve deeper problems. Political and economic systems cannot be fixed as if they are car engines, replacing bad parts with good. A society is an organic whole that is hard to micromanage. Despite their best efforts, aid organizations still struggle to encourage change that is self-sustaining. Monumental gaps in quality of life (as defined by the United Nations to mean access to food, shelter, a livelihood, social stability, health care, and education) still remain.

Ultimately, deep culture does seem to play an important role in how economic and social systems develop, and it can have an important impact on a community's material quality of life. Take the case of the island of Hispaniola in the Caribbean Sea.[4] The western side of the island was colonized primarily by the French, had a large population of slaves, won early independence from France, and became the nation of Haiti. The eastern portion of the island was colonized by the Spanish, had fewer slaves, remained part of Spain longer, and eventually gained independence as the Dominican Republic.

The Dominican Republic, while not a rich country, has developed economically at a pace with the rest of Latin America. Yet Haiti, despite sharing nearly identical geography and having won its political independence first, is one of the poorest countries in the world, ranking extremely low on the United Nations Human Development Index. The difference, it would seem, is the differing cultural histories of the two countries.

So just what are the cultural factors that have made such a difference in this case? It's hard to say. Recent research suggests that certain deep culture values and assumptions, such as the perception of wealth, are related to higher levels of economic output. Is wealth limited, meaning that if some people have more than others have less, or unlimited, meaning that there's no limit to how much can be created? Societies that agree with the former statement tend to be less economically developed. Other deep culture factors may be attitudes toward fate (are humans in control of their own destiny?), or a belief in magic versus an assumption that the physical world only follows natural laws. Values related to the importance of sharing and communal responsibility may contribute to people finding less reason to save and plan for the future.

There is, of course, a chicken-and-egg quality to some of these ideas. Do people feel that wealth is limited because in their society it actually is? Or does that belief somehow inhibit greater economic productivity? There's no single answer to these questions, and deep culture is, at best, one of the factors that leads to large discrepancies in quality-of-life indicators. Still, deep culture constitutes an important part of how humans make sense of their world and is closely related to the kinds of societies we create for ourselves, so it can't be ignored when asking such important questions.

WHAT TO DO

I've painted a depressing picture. Prejudice, ethnic tension, and war still abound. There are whole regions mired in poverty. But let's look for a moment at some reasons for optimism. Technology and economic development have raised the standard of living for large numbers of people. Many people on the planet today have access to greater material wealth than at any time in human history. Globalization is breaking down barriers and has allowed new technologies to penetrate into previously isolated communities. It's not strange for rural African farmers to use cell phones to check commodity prices in order to better negotiate a fair price for their crops.

But clearly there's a lot of work that must be done. Fortunately, globalization has created lots of opportunities to help. We can dedicate time to an organization that is working on some of these problems. We can easily research an area that interests us—microfinancing, education, women's issues, sustainable agriculture, and so on—and find a way to make a contribution. And when you spend time abroad, consider going to less developed countries. While there, seek out local organizations or initiatives that you can support. Be creative. On a trip to Peru, my brother made a point of visiting an elementary school, got to know the principle, and ended up sponsoring a bright student from a poor family.

I don't think that cultural understanding alone solves social or economic problems. But I believe it does make us more empathetic. The difficulties faced by a child growing up in Haiti become more real to us, and the need to look for solutions is felt more urgently. I think cultural understanding also inclines us to seek practical solutions rather than assign blame. It helps us avoid overly simplistic thinking about issues of conflict, prejudice, and war. It prepares us to learn and look at an issue from different points of view. This allows us to be idealists who are also realists.

CHAPTER ELEVEN

Personal Growth *and* Deep Culture Learning

IN 1982, DURING A TRIP through southern Mexico, I met a German man who was selling hand-painted postcards near the beach in Puerto Escondido, Mexico. They were simple water colors, many depicting ocean scenes. When I asked if they represented the nearby beach, he explained that they were actually inspired by things he had seen during more than a year of low-budget travel. Many were the result of the months he spent in Polynesia, where he had been impressed by the changing colors of the sea and women who wear fresh flowers in their hair every day. I was fascinated by his accounts. At the time, he seemed to me the perfect voyager; he fit a set of idealized notions I had about spiritual quests. I fancied him to be a wandering seeker of wisdom.

These days, I have fewer romantic notions about the lessons we learn on our sojourns. I used to think that we learned about the world by seeing exotic places that were "authentic." But if you travel enough you start to see that "exotic" doesn't exist. Authenticity is hard to define, and every place you go is mostly mundane to the people that live there. In a sense, where we travel or decide to live doesn't matter. As I have argued in this book, we learn by responding to adaptive challenges, not by seeking out the wisest cultures or most sacred locations.

Taking a journey requires two decisions. First, we must decide where we will go. We seldom have the freedom to wander as the German traveler did. Sometimes our role in deciding is very limited. Our company may send us abroad or we may emigrate to our partner's home country. Our university may offer a study abroad program in Norway but not Finland. But then, we must also decide (at least at some level) how we will go. What attitudes will we take with us? What are our goals? What do we expect? And how will we react if things don't go as planned?

The German traveler felt that the purpose of a sojourn was to attain a certain state of mind. I agree. So in the final chapter of this introduction to deep culture, let's look at some of the attitudes that we can cultivate that will help us gain intercultural sensitivity and grow as people. It's a list based simply on my experience and on the conversations I've had with others. After that, I'll give you just a few practical tips on finding a sojourn that lends itself to deep learning.

ENGAGEMENT

Some people talk about their travels in terms of "getting away." But while it's true that leaving home gives us a new perspective on our lives, deep culture learning is not something that's done on a beach or in a cave, isolated from experience. We learn from doing and trying new things, meeting new people, exploring new places. It is an active process. If anything, dealing with day-to-day reality in a new place is *more* stressful than life at home. We need to spend more energy just to take care of our daily needs.

This requires a spirit of engagement—a trial-and-error approach to our sojourn. If we try to plan everything out, avoid inconvenience, and cushion ourselves from change, we end up learning less. We must be ready to take chances. The ideal is to care deeply about what we do without being too attached to how things turn out.

For most of us, any attempt to adapt to a new environment brings to light our own self-importance. We are so used to being in control of our personal world that simply being in a new place can create stress and uncertainty. Dealing with people we find unpredictable or unpleasant prick's our pride. A sense of self-importance is a natural part of our human evolution, but deep culture learning requires that we put aside our ego's petty defenses.

The next time your baggage is lost, view it as a challenge to your flexibility. When you struggle with a foreign language, realize that you are attempting to modify communication patterns you've been building for a lifetime, and keep trying. When you find yourself irritated by the "inefficiency" of the locals, recognize that your feelings aren't caused by their behavior, but by your expectations about their behavior. We can't deny our own feelings, but we shouldn't blame them on others. The spirit of engagement means that when things are going badly, we keep trying.

RECONCILIATION

Deep culture learning creates on ongoing series of contradictions that must be reconciled. We participate in a new community, but we don't necessarily belong there. We observe how things are done abroad, and in doing so we gain insight into our home country. We must adapt our behavior yet not lose sight of who we are. We ought to accept others' view of things but must maintain our own perspective. We should engage with other people but shouldn't be pushy. We need to be receptive to others but not passive. We need confidence to face learning challenges with humility.

One historical figure that personifies the engagement and reconciliation of deep culture learning is Mohandas Gandhi. He exhibited great moral clarity, yet still maintained a deeply empathetic and multicultural view of the world. Born in 1869 to Hindu parents, he was raised in a Jain community. At age nineteen, Gandhi went to live in England. A student of world religions and a deeply spiritual person, he was nevertheless deeply involved in the secular world of politics and struggles for social justice. Gandhi transcended apparent contradictions: he was an Indian fighting for independence from England, but he didn't hate the English; he fought for equality but did so without violence; and he deeply respected different religious traditions but maintained his own spiritual path.

Nelson Mandela is also an example of someone who managed to reconcile extreme contradictions in his fight for social justice in South Africa. Throughout the struggle, he never lost sight of the fact that he was not battling whites but rather the apartheid system and the prejudice that it was built on. Mandela managed to hate racism without hating racists. Despite persecution and imprisonment, he maintained a deeply empathetic view of the worldview of whites— to the point of befriending and attempting to educate white guards in prison. However, he was no sellout. Mandela simply understood that the guards' attitudes were often a result of the deep culture assumptions they grew up with. He also knew that no amount of conditioning takes away the ability of the individual to gain new perspectives.

I don't bring up these remarkable individuals because I believe we have to emulate them in particular, or that those who seek deep culture learning should necessarily be politically or socially active. Rather, I think they can give us perspective. While perhaps extremely stressful, the problems we face on our sojourns are usually rather minor. When we feel like complaining or have trouble accepting the people around us, an understanding of the struggles of people like Gandhi and Mandela can remind us to turn adversity into growth. They found their place in an often harsh world and used that struggle to bring out the best in their best nature. We can do that too.

INNER AND OUTER

The engagement and reconciliation of deep culture learning must be cultivated. Naturally, we don't have to be far from home to do so. We face adaptive challenges all the time at work, with our spouse, on a team, or with a new boss. The common thread here is that we must deal with the changing needs and expectation of those around us.

This learning process can be understood in terms of inner and outer practice. *Outer practice* involves the cultivation of openness and curiosity. We strive to be empathetic and learn to look at a situation from the point of view of others. This requires that we withhold personal judgment. Different cultural norms can teach us a new way of being. I learned to open up in Mexico and became a better listener in Japan. African friends have helped me appreciate the importance of family. Time in Vietnam and Nepal showed me how influenced I've been by the cultures of frenetic consumption in Tokyo and California.

Inner practice entails paying attention to what happens inside of us. Our thoughts are often full of criticism and judgments. When we feel threatened, our bodies react with defensiveness, anger, and irritation. *Bodymindfulness*—an awareness of our physical and emotional states—can help us notice these reactions.[1] But we shouldn't judge ourselves too harshly. Being hypercritical of oneself only creates a new round of judgments. The goal of awareness is not a heavy-handed attempt to change ourselves but a desire for self-understanding. This can help us to gently let go of the reactions that we discover are not useful.

BREAKING ROUTINES

Our lives are often dominated by routine. We tend to eat the same foods, hang out with the same people, and go to the same places. We drive our car and pet the dog without active awareness of what we're doing. And that can be a good thing; allowing our cognitive unconscious autopilot to manage our lives gives us stability and frees up our mind to think about other things. After all, we don't want to think about stepping on the brake every time we pull up to a stop sign.

Yet routine can deaden our lives. When I first traveled in Mexico, I was surprised to discover chili-and-lime-flavored potato chips. The fact that I even remember this speaks to the power of breaking those routines. Confounded expectations force us to become aware of what we are doing and help us learn from our environment.

A sojourn forcefully breaks the routines of everyday life. In a new environment, an endless number of things require active attention. This demand can be tiring and provoke irritation or frustration. In England, I found that my American sense of humor didn't serve me well. The routine way I was used to expressing my personality had to be set aside. In Tokyo, I had to learn to be comfortable with silence. With my Mexican girlfriend, I was forced to examine my routine assumptions about what it meant to be a good boyfriend.

Intentionally breaking routines can be good training for deep culture learning. Order a dish that you've never tried. Take a different route home. Switch the hand that you use to hold your fork. Put your bag on the opposite shoulder. Even these simple disruptions can be quite challenging. The goal is not so much to modify the way we do things, but to become aware of our limited tolerance for change.

The cognitive unconscious can also turn the most exotic experience into a routine. The miracle of jet travel, for example, soon seems humdrum to frequent travelers. When living abroad, we may find a niche and stop learning. Some sojourners live for years abroad and never become competent at speaking the local language. Catching ourselves before we fall into deadening routines can help us avoid these pitfalls.

PLANNING THE JOURNEY

A deep culture sojourn is different from a spiritual journey or quest. In many ways, these types of journeys are diametrically opposed. A spiritual journey seeks an ideal, whereas deep culture travel seeks to understand the hidden assumptions behind our ideals. A spiritual journey seeks to transcend the world of everyday affairs whereas deep culture travel revels in the details of everyday life in another place. A spiritual journey seeks universal truths that can be shared across cultures and, indeed, across the ages. The deep culture sojourner seeks the relative truths of many different people and places and uses them to construct new understandings.

The guiding principal for a deep culture sojourn is to *go local*. It's anti-exotic. This doesn't mean that we shouldn't see famous sights, but that we should seek out the experiences and point of view of people who live in the place we are visiting. This often requires concerted effort; the conveniences of globalization can insulate us from local life and attitudes. This doesn't necessarily mean *living* abroad. One of the most powerful short deep culture experiences I've had was attending a Sunday service at a black Southern Baptist church while I was in Louisiana. I was in my own country, but in another world.

Many of us would like to have a longer, more involved experience abroad but lack the time or resources. In this case, the focus for planning a sojourn shifts to making the most out of one's limited time away. It's hard to connect with a local community if you will be staying only a few days or weeks, but there are some shortcuts to going local for a short time:

- *Couch surfing* is a movement centered around local residents offering free accommodation to travelers.
- WWOOFing (World Wide Opportunities on Organic Farms) is an international network in which travelers exchange volunteer work on organic farms in exchange for room and board.
- Social networking sites—there are people in other countries who want to meet people like you. Spend some time finding them before departing.
- There are many specialized adventure and cultural tours that list their itineraries online. You don't have to sign up—you can just use the information for trip planning. Organize a trip around a theme (like his-

tory, wine, or live music) that will give a focus to your interactions with locals.

* Transitions abroad is a web portal that provides resources for cultural travel and international living. It focuses on the deeper side of foreign experiences.

LANGUAGE LEARNING

Like it or not, learning to speak a foreign language well and using it to function in another society is a powerful deep culture learning experience. Few people achieve a truly high level of deep culture understanding without having learned a foreign language. Language offers us a window into the worldview of another cultural community.

Less proficient speakers of foreign languages tend to think that communicating information accurately is the measure of one's ability, and this can certainly be a challenge. Simply learning your first 500 vocabulary words in a new language can be a Herculean task. But learning a language does more than allow you to shop and explain things, it also gives access to the mental world of people who speak that language. My first real interest in language learning developed when I was a teenager. I worked at the main gate of a theme park in Southern California that frequently had Spanish-speaking guests. I had the sense that they were visitors from another world. As I learned Spanish, a door opened to that world. This led me to my encounter with Antonio. When I then went to live in Mexico, I immersed myself into this new way of life.

Native English speakers may underestimate the importance of learning a foreign language. We are often too used to others learning our language and may unconsciously depend too much on the deference afforded by the powerful position of English. Many native English speakers are poor at speaking international English (a more standardized form of English that is easy for non-native speakers to understand). Learning a foreign language can help us avoid this.

Language learning is a humbling experience. You must put up with feelings of frustration and inadequacy. If you do business in a foreign language, you may feel that you are boxing with one hand tied behind your back. To use a foreign language to fall in love, make friends, meet in-laws, or find a job requires adjusting deeply to another view of the world. It pushes you to a level of cultural adaptation that is rare if you stick to your native language. Cultural learning is a trial-and-error process, and few things demand as much trial and error as learning a new language.

ENTRY POINT

I used to be impressed by people who had visited many different countries. But business travelers who see mostly conference rooms or backpackers who visit twenty countries in six months often spend much of their time skimming over the surface of the worlds they visit. The more impressive challenge of a deep culture sojourn is the ability to find an "entry point"—a way to connect with people in a new place. Antonio was an entry point for me into life in Mexico. With this in mind I have also taken part in language study that included a homestay, studied African dance, found an expatriate job, and done home exchanges. The key is to connect a need or interest that you have with people in a new community.

For a longer stay, it can be helpful to cultivate cultural "informants"—people who can help you negotiate the ins and outs of the community. In Mexico, my girlfriend helped me understand how to get things done and manage my business. In Japan, I was at first overwhelmed trying to negotiate the complex web of relationships I encountered as a tenured faculty in a Japanese university. I could not keep up or defend myself in the face of complicated institutional politics. But by biding my time, and discretely asking lots of questions, I eventually connected to colleagues who supported and helped me. In Paris, I similarly befriended a Senegalese teacher of German who had a lot of experience with fitting into French life.

We often think of a journey as beginning with our departure. But a deep culture journey starts with our entrance into a new reality. My conversations with Antonio served as the entry point for all of the cultural learning I've done in the past twenty-five years. I owe him a tremendous debt of gratitude. Unfortunately, I've lost touch with him, so I can't thank him for inviting me into his world. Instead, I've tried to share his story with you in the writing of this book. I hope that this contributes in some small way to greater deep culture learning and serves as a tribute to the lessons that began for me on the streets of Ensenada so many years ago.

Deep Culture
Learning
Profiler

A quick-reference guide to the cultural learning process as explained in chapter 8.

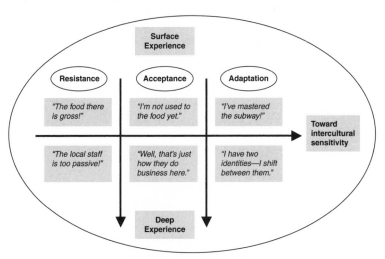

The cultural learning process: Helps visualize the cultural learning process using statements about cultural difference

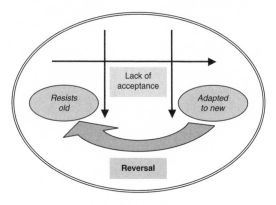

Reversal: Rejection of the home cultural community in favor of the new one

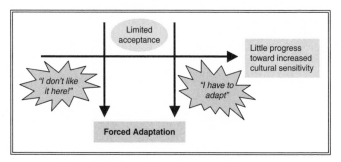

Forced adaptation: The psychological conflict caused by adapting and resisting at the same time

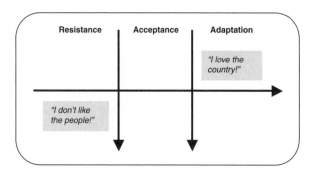

Mixed reactions: Multiple and often contradictory reactions to our experiences

FURTHER READING

The foundational readings of deep culture begin with *The Silent Language* and *Beyond Culture* by Edward T. Hall.[1] In these works, Hall focuses on hidden systematic cultural differences, particularly those dealing with time and the use of space. Hall created some of the first formal terminology to compare elements of deep culture, such as high– versus low-context communication and polychronic and monochronic time.

If you'd like to go back a bit earlier, read the enjoyable *Coming of Age in Samoa* by Margaret Mead.[2] First published in 1928, it recounts her experiences studying Samoan adolescents, and includes discussion on sexual mores and gender roles. It created a sensation when it was published because it challenged American cultural assumptions. Mead was only twenty-three when she went to Samoa and twenty-seven when her book was published. Be aware that her observations about Samoa have since been seriously questioned. Lacking an understanding of evolutionary psychologists, she probably overestimated the degree to which culture shapes human behavior. Mead studied with the legendary Franz Boas, a pioneer of modern anthropology. She also studied with Ruth Benedict, a student of Boas and anthropology pioneer who wrote the classic *Patterns of Cultures*.[3]

If you are interested in understanding patterns of cultural difference, I recommend *Riding the Waves of Culture* by Trompenaars and Hampden-Turner.[4] Though it is written with a no-nonsense business audience in mind, it has intellectual depth. Trompenaars and Hampden-Turner have been influenced by dilemma theory and look at culture as a series of solutions to the challenges of social organization. If you are mostly interested in making sense of the cultural difference you find when abroad, this book is a good place to start.

If you want a detailed (and rather academic) look at the process of adapting to cultural difference, you might pick up a copy of *Deep Culture: The Hidden Challenges of Global Living* (Shaules).[5] It introduces a series of expatriates who talk about their cultural learning experiences. These are used as the starting point for describing a model of deep culture learning. The book analyzes questions such as, "How is it that some people live abroad for years without having deep culture experiences?" and "How can we interpret what people say about their deep culture experiences?"

For a genetics perspective of human evolution, including discussions of the development of language and culture, I recommend *Before the Dawn: Recovering the Lost History of Our Ancestors* by Nicholas Wade.[6] You will learn, among other things, how geneticists have been able to figure out when humans started wearing clothes, how many people were in the group of humans who left Africa and spread throughout the rest of the planet, and the length of time it took for humans to crowd out Neanderthals and—perhaps—push them into extinction.

The explosion of culture that happened approximately 50,000 years ago is perhaps the single most important event in human history. For an easy-to-read account of how that may have happened, try reading *The Dawn of Human Culture*, by Richard Klein with Blake Edgar.[7] Klein is an advocate of the idea that culture developed over a relatively short period of time.

If you are interested in the brain and the cognitive unconscious, I highly recommend *Strangers to Ourselves*, by Timothy D. Wilson.[8] It discusses the many ways that Freud's view of the unconscious is at odds with current research among cognitive scientists. This book can be a bit scary because as you read it you start to understand just how much our unconscious mind shapes our experiences. Could it be that our conscious mind is simply explaining to ourselves the decisions that the cognitive unconscious has already made?

For a view of how unconscious cognitive processes are affected by culture, read *The Geography of Thought*, by Richard Nisbett.[9] A psychologist, Nisbett introduces a great deal of research to support his argument that culture affects cognition in fundamental ways. The research that I introduced with the cow, chicken, and grass image comes from this book.

For a look into the question of how the brain produces consciousness, pick up a copy of *The Feeling of What Happens: Body and Emotion in the Making of Consciousness* by Antonio Damasio.[10] Questions about consciousness are often asked by philosophers, but neurologists are starting to understand the functioning of the brain well enough to guess at how it is produced. Understanding this process can help us understand how both the cognitive unconscious and the narrative conscious work.

Another book that deals with consciousness is *The Embodied Mind* by Varela, Thompson, and Rosch.[11] The authors examine consciousness from the perspective of cognitive science and compare those ideas with the Buddhist understanding of perception. They argue that the Buddhist view of how our mind produces our experience accords well with the recent findings of cognitive scientists. This book is not a light read and was published back in 1993, but it is a brilliant synthesis of Western and Eastern ideas about cognition. Of particular interest to me was the discussion of consciousness as an emergent property.

Deep culture is not, of course, just about academic study. It's also an attempt to understand our own lives and take responsibility for our decisions. My view of the human capacity to take responsibility for our decisions has been heavily influenced by Carlos Castaneda. His book, *Journey to Ixtlan*, discusses practices that use the mundane events of everyday life as the fuel for transformative learning.[12] He discusses losing self-importance, assuming responsibility, using death as an advisor, "not doing," and more. Some say that Castaneda was an enlightened shaman, while others call him a charlatan. It doesn't matter; there is a highly practical element to his work that I find both inspiring and useful.

Deep culture can be seen at the macro level of society as well. A book that ignited a firestorm of debate about the role of culture in international conflict is *The Clash of Civilizations and the Remaking of World Order*, by Samuel P. Huntington.[13] When reading this book, I often felt that what Huntington was calling "civilization" could be better called *deep culture*. The book revolves around the argument that unconscious elements of culture are powerful forces that can lead to conflict and that these must be understood to solve the problems we face in our globalized world.

Economists have been looking at the question of how cultural values shape economic development. The book *Culture Matters: How Values Shape Human Progress*, edited by Lawrence El Harrison and Samuel P. Huntington, takes on this subject empirically without being cowed by taboos about associating economic development with culture.[14] In the appendix, there is a spirited written exchange between an African development specialist accused of elitism by a Western anthropologist for considering certain cultural values as "problems" to be overcome. Their debate is full of deep culture lessons.

One book that does a brilliant job of deconstructing deep culture patterns in Japan is *The Anatomy of Dependence* by Takeo Doi.[15] It analyzes only a single Japanese word— *amae* (dependence)—but shows how this concept is a central organizing principal of the Japanese worldview. This book is valuable not only as a way to understand Japan, but as a tour-de-force of deep culture awareness on the part of the author. When I read this, I find myself thinking I could never explain the inner workings of American deep culture values with such an impressive degree of insight.

A book that describes the deep culture of the United States is *American Cultural Patterns: A Cross-cultural Perspective*, by Stewart and Bennett.[16] Though first written in 1972 by Stewart, it still holds up very well (thanks in part to later contributions from Bennett). It describes, for example, patterns of language and nonverbal behavior, forms of social relations, perception of the world, and perception of the self. Though it may be useful for visitors to the United States, I especially recommend it for Americans. You will find yourself nodding your head in recognition of cultural patterns that you feel intuitively but that are difficult to articulate.

The works listed here give a glimpse of deep culture from differing perspectives. Intercultural specialists may notice that there are few books listed here from the field of intercultural communication, and none by some of the giants in that field. I also haven't included books from the vast literature that deals with cultural identity and cultural marginality. It's not that I don't see value in these other works, but simply that the books I've listed have been some of the most useful for helping me get a handle on deep culture as a *lived experience* rather than as a field of academic study or as a literary pursuit. I hope you find them useful in your cultural adventures.

You can contact the author and find resources related to deep culture at *www.deepculture.org.*

NOTES

Chapter One

1. There is no single agreed-upon term for the unconscious cultural patterns that I refer to in this book. What I am calling deep culture is perhaps most often referred to as *out-of-awareness culture*, or *implicit culture*. Edward Hall first drew attention to the out-of-awareness nature of our cultural programming in his classic 1959 book *The Silent Language*. Hall is a primary inspiration for me, and I like to think of this book as a contribution to his legacy. Edward Stewart started using the term deep culture well before I did.

Chapter Two

1. The expression "programming of the mind" comes from Hofstede (1997). Among intercultural specialists, the concept of culture existing and functioning at the unconscious level is widely accepted, as exemplified in the widely used iceberg metaphor—with the largest part below the surface. There is no broad agreement on a single definition of deep culture. My working definition is, deep culture is the (primarily) out-of-awareness patterns of meaning that serve as the organizational schema for one's cultural worldview. Cultural worldview refers to the shared frameworks of meaning and interpretation that communities use to mediate social interaction. Like language, deep culture is an evolving and emergent property that cannot be fully represented by the knowledge or

behavior of any single individual. It exists only as an abstraction at the level of group interaction. Deep cultural patterns exist both within the individual as systematic meanings and competencies, and within the patterns of interaction among individuals within a community.

2. The terminology I use in the onion metaphor comes largely from the work of Trompenaars and Hampden-Turner (1998).

Chapter Three

1. The term *group intelligence* most often refers to the phenomena of people converging on a common understanding of something. I am using it more broadly to mean the ability of a large group of people to accomplish something (like creating a complex society) that is beyond the capacity of any single individual to plan or fully understand. One well-studied example is *creolization*, when the children of speakers of pidgin languages create a newly formed language—a creole—spontaneously through their interaction.

2. Also called the *adaptive unconscious*. See Wilson (2002).

3. A major symposium sponsored by Harvard University's Academy for International and Area Studies examined the relationship between culture and economic development. See Harrison and Huntington (2000).

4. A great deal has been researched and published in areas such as cultural differences as related to business, culture shock, and intercultural training for expatriates and managers. See, for example, J. Bennett (1998); M. J. Bennett (1986); Black (1988); Brislin (1981); Byram, Nichols, and Stevens (2001); Dinges and Lieberman (1989); Goldstein and Smith (1999); Hall and Hall (1987); Hannigan (1990); Hofstede (1980, 1983, 1997); Landis and Bhagat (1996); Oberg (1960); Shaules (2004); Stoorti (1994); Trompenaars and Hampden-Turner (1998); Valdes (1995); Ward, Okura, Kennedy, and Kojima (1998); Weaver (1993).

5. See, for example, the work of Clotaire Rapaille (2006), a consultant specializing in the use of deep culture associations in advertising campaigns.
6. See Luna, Ringberg, and Peracchio (2008).

Chapter Four

1. The dates in this chapter are approximate. There isn't enough consensus among specialists to create a conclusive timeline. The larger point is that deep culture is a product of our evolutionary biology.
2. For an examination of the biological bases of consciousness, I recommend the work of Antonio Damasio (1999). Not everyone agrees that consciousness as I describe it is a big deal. The linguist Steven Pinker has written in great detail about human cognitive capabilities, yet dismisses this kind self-referential thought as "navel gazing." See Pinker (1997), p. 123.
3. There has been very interesting research into the question of whether certain animals have a "theory of mind"—that is, whether they realize that others experience the world from a different perspective than they do. Results show that some animals do. A chimp may, for example, mislead other chimps in order to prevent them from discovering a hidden treat. This shows that the chimp understands at some level the workings of the minds of other chimps. My assertion that humans and animals experience the world differently isn't meant to deny this. My point is that the way that humans live "in our heads" in a conceptual world is very different from animal cognition.
4. See Wade (2006).
5. There are multiple theories of how cultural evolution takes place. For an account of how *memes* (a unit of culture such as symbols, knowledge, or practices) may spread through populations in much the same way that genetic variation does,

see Dawkins (2006). For an account of a Darwinian theory of cultural evolution, see Richerson and Boyd (2005).

Chapter Five

1. For more about this period in Boas' life see Cole (1999).
2. He proposed that no cultural community is more advanced than another, and that to learn about other cultural communities we must learn to understand them on their own terms. This insight encouraged a systematic, less judgmental approach to studying culture. His approach to the systematic study of culture became the basis for American anthropology's division into the categories of physical anthropology, archaeology, linguistics, and cultural anthropology.
3. See Mead (1961).
4. The Sapir-Whorf hypothesis has provoked endless controversy since it was first proposed. At issue is to what degree language influences our perceptions of the world. Many studies have been done, for example, on whether having more or fewer color words in a language effects our ability to perceive colors (the short answer is: not really). It's easy to get bogged down in the details of claims and counterclaims. One limitation of much research in this area is that it often focuses on simple word-level meanings, such as colors or shapes. It's important to distinguish between the word *perception* in the limited sense of categorizing elements in our physical environment from *perception* used to mean one's view of a particular subject. People from different cultural communities may or may not perceive colors or shapes differently, but they certainly have different perceptions about what is normal and fair in human relations and interaction. As discussed in chapter 6, cognitive scientists are currently studying how culture influences basic cognitive processes. In my mind, this kind of research is of more immediate relevance to deep culture learners.
5. Luna et al. (2008).

6. Hall (1976), p. 240.
7. Hall (1976), p. 213.
8. Hofstede's categories of cultural comparison are high versus low power distance, individualism versus collectivism, masculinity versus femininity, high versus low uncertainty avoidance, and long– versus short-term orientation. See Hofstede (1983, 1997).
9. See, for example, Wilson (2002).
10. See, for example, Coleman (2006).
11. Damasio (1999).
12. Wade (2006).

Chapter Six

1. Confucius's ideas were also a product of the social environment he lived in. There is a chicken-and-egg quality to any attempt to discuss the influence of ancient thinkers. For an account of Confucius in the context of his time, see Chin (2007).
2. The material in this section comes largely from Nisbett (2003).
3. From Nisbett (2003).
4. Wilson (2002) uses the term *adaptive unconscious*. Others use the term *cognitive unconscious*.

Chapter Seven

1. You can visit Ludovic's blog at *www.sekoyamag.com/ludovichubler*.
2. Yuko is not her real name. You can read about this woman in Shaules (2007).
3. See M. J. Bennett (1993), p. 24. Key to this definition is the concept of *differentiation*, which Bennett uses to mean both the variety of ways that people differentiate phenomena and also the broader patterns of differentiations, or worldviews, that people have.

4. Bennett see cultural learning as developmental, meaning that it takes place over time and involves an increase in particular cognitive capacities. He divides this learning process into three ethnocentric stages (*denial*, *defense*, and *minimization*) and three ethnorelative stages (*acceptance*, *adaptation*, and *integration*).

5. The concept of a positive cultural marginality was first discussed in detail by Adler (1977), who used the term *multicultural man*. Milton Bennett's Developmental Model of Intercultural Sensitivity labels the final stage of ethnorelative thinking as *integration*, which includes the idea of the integrated marginality. See M. J. Bennett (1993). Janet Bennett (J. Bennett, 1993) has written insightfully about marginality in her work on cultural transitions.

6. See de Nooy and Hanna (2003).

7. You can learn more and try implicit association tests here: *https://implicit.harvard.edu/implicit*.

8. J. Bennett (1993).

Chapter Eight

1. For a full description of the terms used to describe cultural learning in this chapter, including, *resistance*, *acceptance*, *adaptation*, *dislike*, *surface*, *deep*, *mixed reactions*, and *demand for change*, see Shaules (2007).

2. I am paraphrasing this statement from Milton Bennett. I have heard him use different iterations of this when speaking at conferences and workshops. This isn't an exact quote, but I hope that it captures the essence of his point.

Chapter Nine

1. Clyde Kluckhohn saw culture in terms of value orientations toward five key areas of life: (1) human nature, (2) man/nature,

(3) time, (4) activity, and (5) social relations. See Kluckhohn and Strodbeck (1961).

2. Trompenaars and Hampden-Turner elaborate on seven orientations: (1) universalism/collectivism, (2) particularism/universalism, (3) affective/neutral, (4) specific/diffuse, (5) inner/outer control, (6) ascribed/achieved status, and (7) synchronic/sequential time. See Trompenaars and Hampden-Turner (1998).

Chapter Ten

1. Huntington (1996).
2. Shergill, Frith, and Wolpert (2003).
3. See Weber (2001).
4. This example is taken from Harrison and Huntington (2000).

Chapter Eleven

1. *Mindfulness* is a Buddhist term that refers to living more in the present moment so as to become more aware of the inner and outer elements of our experience. *Bodymindfulness* is a term used by Nagata (2000) to refer to an awareness of our physical states as a tool for personal growth.

Further Readings

1. Hall (1959) and Hall (1976), respectively.
2. Mead (1961).
3. Benedict (1934).
4. Trompenaars and Hampden-Turner (1998).
5. Shaules (2007).
6. Wade (2006).
7. Klein and Edgar (2002).

8. Wilson (2002).
9. Nisbett (2003).
10. Damasio (1999).
11. Varela, Thompson, and Rosch (1995).
12. Castaneda (1974).
13. Huntington (1996).
14. Harrison and Huntington (2000).
15. Doi (1995).
16. Stewart and Bennett (1991).

REFERENCES

Adler, P. S. (1977). Beyond cultural identity: Reflections upon cultural and multicultural man. In R. Brislin (Ed.), *Culture learning: Concepts, application and research* (pp. 56–75). Honolulu: University Press of Hawaii.

Benedict, R. (1934). *Patterns of culture*. Boston: Houghton Mifflin.

Bennett, J. (1993). Cultural marginality: Identity issues in intercultural training. In M. R. Paige (Ed.), *Education for the intercultural experience* (pp. 109–35). Yarmouth, ME: Intercultural Press.

Bennett, J. (1998). Transition shock: Putting culture shock in perspective. In M. J. Bennett (Ed.), *Basic concepts of intercultural communication*. Yarmouth, ME: Intercultural Press.

Bennett, M. J. (1986). A developmental approach to training for intercultural sensitivity. *International Journal of Intercultural Relations, 10*, 179–200.

Bennett, M. J. (1993). Towards ethnorelativism: A developmental model of intercultural sensitivity. In M. R. Paige (Ed.), *Education for the intercultural experience* (pp. 21–71). Yarmouth, ME: Intercultural Press.

Black, J. S. (1988). Work role transitions: A study of American expatriate managers in Japan. *Journal of International Business Studies, 19*, 277–94.

Brislin, R. (1981). *Cross-cultural encounters*. New York: Pergamon.

References

Byram, M., Nichols, A., & Stevens, D. (Eds.). (2001). *Developing intercultural competence in practice.* Clevedon, UK: Multilingual Matters.

Castaneda, C. (1974). *Journey to Ixtlan.* New York: Pocket Books.

Chin, A. (2007). *The authentic Confucius: A Life of thought and politics.* New York: Scribner.

Cole, D. (1999). *Franz Boas: The early years, 1858–1906.* Seattle: University of Washington Press.

Coleman, D. (2006). *Social intelligence: The new science of human relationships.* New York: Bantam Books.

Damasio, A. (1999). *The feeling of what happens: Body and emotion in the making of consciousness.* New York: Harcourt.

Dawkins, R. (2006). *The selfish gene* (3rd ed.). Oxford, UK: Oxford University Press.

de Nooy, J., & Hanna, B. (2003). Cultural information gathering by Australian students in France. *Language and Intercultural Communication, 3*(1), 64–80.

Dinges, N. G., & Lieberman, D. A. (1989). Intercultural communication competence: Coping with stressful work situations. *International Journal of Intercultural Relations, 13,* 371–85.

Doi, T. (1995). *Anatomy of dependence.* Tokyo: Kodansha International.

Goldstein, D. L., & Smith, D. H. (1999). The analysis of the effects of experiential training on sojourners' cross-cultural adaptability. *International Journal of Intercultural Relations, 28*(1), 157–73.

Hall, E. T. (1959). *The silent language.* New York: Anchor Books.

Hall, E. T. (1976). *Beyond culture.* New York: Anchor Books Doubleday.

Hall, E. T., & Hall, M. R. (1987). *Hidden differences: Doing business with the Japanese.* New York: Anchor Books Doubleday.

Hannigan, T. P. (1990). Traits, attitudes, and skills that are related to intercultural effectiveness and their implications for cross-cultural training: A review of the literature. *International Journal of Intercultural Relations, 14*(1), 89–111.

Harrison, L. E., & Huntington, S. P. (Eds.). (2000). *Culture matters: How values shape human progress*. New York: Basic Books.

Hofstede, G. (1980). *Culture's consequences: International differences in work-related values*. Beverly Hills, CA: Sage.

Hofstede, G. (1983). Dimensions of national culture in fifty countries and three regions. In J. B. Deregowski, S. Dziurawiec, & R. C. Annis (Eds.), *Expiscations in cross-cultural psychology* (pp. 335–55). Lisse, Netherlands: Swetz & Zeitlinger.

Hofstede, G. (1997). *Cultures and organizations: Software of the mind*. New York: McGraw-Hill.

Huntington, S. P. (1996). *The clash of civilizations and the remaking of world order*. New York: Simon & Schuster.

Klein, R. G., with Edgar, B. (2002). *The dawn of human culture*. New York: Wiley.

Kluckhohn, F., & Strodbeck, F. (1961). *Variations in value orientations*. New York: Harper & Row.

Landis, D., & Bhagat, R. S. (Eds.). (1996). *Handbook of intercultural training* (2nd ed.). Thousand Oaks, CA: Sage.

Luna, D., Ringberg, T., & Peracchio, L. A. (2008). One Individual, two identities: Frame switching among biculturals. *Journal of Consumer Research, 35*(2), 279–93.

Mead, M. (1961). *Coming of age in Samoa*. New York: Perennial Classics.

Nagata, A. L. (2000). Resonant connections. *ReVision, 22*(4), 24–30.

Nisbett, R. E. (2003). *The geography of thought*. New York: Free Press.

Oberg, K. (1960). Culture shock: Adjustment to new cultural environments. *Practical Anthropology, 7*, 177–82.

Pinker, S. (1997). *How the mind works*. New York: Norton.

Rapaille, C. (2006). *The culture code*. New York: Broadway Books.

Richerson, P. J., & Boyd, R. (2005). *Not by genes alone: How culture transformed human evolution*. Chicago: University of Chicago Press.

Shaules, J. (2004). *Explicit and implicit cultural difference in cultural learning among long-term expatriates.* Southampton, UK: University of Southampton.

Shaules, J. (2007). *Deep culture: The hidden challenges of global living.* Clevedon, UK: Multilingual Matters.

Shergill, S. S., Bays, P. M., Frith, C. D., & Wolpert, D. M. (2003). Two eyes for an eye: The neuroscience of force escalation. *Science, 301,* 187.

Stewart, E. C., & Bennett, M. J. (1991). *American cultural patterns: A cross-cultural perspective.* Yarmouth, ME: Intercultural Press.

Stoorti, C. (1994). *Cross-cultural dialogues.* Yarmouth, ME: Intercultural Press.

Trompenaars, F., & Hampden-Turner, C. (1998). *Riding the waves of culture.* New York: McGraw-Hill.

Valdes, J. M. (1995). *Training know-how for cross cultural and diversity trainers.* Duncanville: Adult Learning Systems.

Varela, F. J., Thompson, E., & Rosch, E. (1995). *The embodied mind: Cognitive science and human experience.* Cambridge: MIT Press.

Wade, N. (2006). *Before the dawn: Recovering the lost history of our ancestors.* New York: Penguin Press.

Ward, C., Okura, Y., Kennedy, A., & Kojima, T. (1998). The U-Curve on trial: A longitudinal study of psychological and sociocultural adjustment during cross-cultural transition. *International Journal of Intercultural Relations, 22*(3), 277–91.

Weaver, G. (1993). Understanding and coping with cross-cultural adjustment stress. In R. M. Page (Ed.), *Education for the intercultural experience* (pp. 137–68).Yarmouth, ME: Intercultural Press.

Weber, M. (2001). *The Protestant ethic and the spirit of capitalism.* London: Routledge Classics.

Wilson, T. D. (2002). *Strangers to ourselves: Discovering the adaptive unconscious.* Cambridge, MA: Belknap Press.

CREDITS

2.1 Ai Ichinomiya

2.2 Ai Ichinomiya

2.3 Ai Ichinomiya

3.1 Ai Ichinomiya

3.2 Ai Ichinomiya

3.3 Fundraw.com at www.fundraw.com/clipart/clip-art/00003218/
Male-Face-Cartoon-Glasses-Slightly-Surprised/

4.1 Wikipedia at http://en.wikipedia.org/wiki/File:BBC-
artefacts.jpg. Image copyright held by author, Chris Hen-
shilwood. Photo by HenningSource. Permission CC-BY-2.5.
Released under the GNU Free Documentation License.

4.2 Wikipedia at http://commons.wikimedia.org/wiki/File:
Metkrok_av_ben_fr%C3%A5n_sten%C3%A5ldern,_
funnen_i_Sk%C3%A5ne.jpg

5.1 Wikipedia at http://commons.wikimedia.org/wiki/File:
FranzBoas.jpg. Photograph from the collection of the
Canadian Museum of Civilization.

5.2 Wikipedia at http://commons.wikimedia.org/wiki/File:
Exposition_universelle_1900.jpg

5.3 Wikipedia at http://en.wikipedia.org/wiki/File:Ota_Benga_
at_Bronx_Zoo.jpg

6.1 Free Clipart Graphics at www.freeclipartnow.com/
religion-mythology/chinese/Confucius.jpg.html

6.2 Ai Ichinomiya

6.3 http://commons.wikimedia.org/wiki/File:Yin_and_Yang.
svg#file

Credits

6.4 Ai Ichinomiya
7.1 Ai Ichinomiya
11UN Ai Ichinomiya
Appendix Ai Ichinomiya

INDEX